Gluten Free Family Recipes
by KOB

Copyright ©2023 by Teresa Anderson. The book author, Teresa Anderson, retains sole copyright to their contributions to this book. All rights reserved.

The Family Cookbook Project provided layout designs and graphical elements are copyright Family Cookbook Project, LLC, 2023. This book was created using the FamilyCookbookProject.com software app.

Teresa Anderson retains sole copyright for her contributions to this book.

Family Cookbook Project - Helping families collect cherished recipes forever.

Visit us on the Web at www.familycookbookproject.com

Our hearts know that we are home because of the tastes and smells that flow from the kitchen... and of course all the people that love us that live within those walls!

I have enjoyed revamping and changing both the old and new recipes to be excellent gluten free baked goods that have great texture and taste. Thank you to everyone who has inspired me to put all of our family favourites into one book to enjoy.

May you enjoy the recipes. My hope is that it inspires you to cook even more of your tradition's gluten-free style.

Enjoy!

ISBN: 9781739005702

Author and Photographer Teresa Anderson

Published by Teresa Anderson

June 2023

A cataloguing record of this book is available from Library and Archives Canada.

 If you need some extra help with techniques and would like someone to *show* you how to bake gluten free, check out my online video classes or if you want to get my Christmas cookbook ... then scan the QR code.

www.glutenfreeKOB.com

A Bit About Me ...

I'm a celiac & I am married to my best friend, who happens to be a dairy free type one diabetic. I am also a mom to two fabulous people. One is a celiac and the other is not (she prides herself as being the 'normal' one in the family!). Our family has a few dietary restrictions, yet I don't think any of us really notice…most days! It's just our 'normal'. Of course, food IS part of our daily life, but it doesn't rule our life. I hope what I've figured out along the way can help you.

My doctor said that she believed I was a celiac since childhood, due to the damage. Yet, I had never heard the word Celiac until I was an adult. The day that I was diagnosed, my doctor scared me to death with her chat about what could happen if I continued to eat gluten. Her words stuck with me, & I've never eaten gluten again!

I grew up with a dad who got up at 4 am to bake every morning, for about 50 years! He was a professional glutenated baker. When I was a child, I would walk into the bakery, & the ladies behind the counter would let me pick any mouthwatering donut I liked. Of course, I picked the biggest one I could find!

When I was first diagnosed, I really needed my doctor's words in my head to keep me from eating gluten (like a soft gooey, Boston cream, donut!). Her words helped me to be able to walk away from ordering a donut with my Tim Hortons coffee. Or saying, 'no thank you' when my extended family gathered & ate cinnamon buns around the kitchen table. Or smile politely when a friend or family member made fun of my gluten-free food, never thinking that I didn't have a choice about this gluten free diet, & that this wasn't a fad diet for me. It was hard in the beginning, & I appreciated my doctor's fear tactic. It worked for me.

When our son was also diagnosed with Celiac, I had a desire to learn how to bake gluten free. I did not want my boy to lose the taste of home. He really was my inspiration to learn!

I read a lot of books, cookbooks, blogs, I took courses, and I began to understand the chemistry behind gluten-free baking. My background in dietary technology was also helpful and made me want to add nutrition wherever I could.

Over the years, I have adopted my grandmas, moms, sisters, friends, and mother-in-law's old family recipes to be gluten-free style! I have enjoyed revamping and changing all the new recipes to make the baked goods have excellent texture and taste. I no longer have any desire for gluten, and I have not for a long time. BUT if you are finding it hard … I hope the recipes and tips shared help you enjoy eating baked goods again!

Bread and muffins do not have to crumble, and gluten-free food does taste good! My family and I enjoy the food we eat very much.

I'm glad you've grabbed a cookbook. I hope you take the time to learn some techniques and tips, and you'll be equipped to carry on some of your old traditions' gluten free style.

Watch one of my baking videos online, follow me on www.glutenfreekob.blog or social media to learn some tips and bake some great foods. I hope you are successful at baking gluten free and carrying on traditions in your home.

I use ingredients that are not hard to find, the baked goods taste excellent and the recipes are not complicated, **YOU CAN DO IT!**

By the way, many people seem to get confused on how to say Gluten Free KOB. KOB rhymes with BOB! And KOB stands for 'Kid Okay'd Bakery'. My celiac, non-celiac and their friends have okayed the baking!

Hope you join me baking online or grab a book and enjoy it as much as myself.

Enjoy!

This Book is dedicated to my family …

I want to thank my family for encouraging me to not give up on trying to cook our traditional family recipes in a new way. When celiac disease entered our family, baking and cooking with ingredients that I had never heard of before was not always easy and to say the least was challenging.

My husband, Mike, I thank you for your wonderful attitude on this journey. You've laughed with me when I had cooking disasters. What's even more amazing is that you ATE the disasters, without complaint! Thank you for being willing to taste test my baking and believing in my dreams of farmers markets, baking classes and cookbooks. I think you are the only one who truly understands how much JOY it brings me to make a little celiac smile over a GOOD gluten free baked item. Thank you for being my biggest fan!

Daniel and Emily, I enjoy cooking for and with you in our home. Family traditions, celebrations and ordinary days all start in the kitchen. The smells of home warm the heart and make you know that you are surrounded by love. I hope you cook from this book through the years and bring the smells and tastes of home to your family, friends and generations to come.

Remember to always add a secret ingredient … A PINCH OF LOVE … and every recipe will turn out just fine. If the recipe did not turn out 'like Mom use to make' … choose to laugh … then dip it in a glass of milk or a cup of coffee … as you don't want to waste those good ingredients! … and enjoy the ones you love around the table. Try again next time!

Daniel and Emily, when you are grown, remember you can always come home to cook or just eat … your Mom ALWAYS has time to share your favourite meal or treat as we forget the world for a while … enjoying each other … surrounded in the smells and tastes home.

Enjoy!

Love, Mom xo

Table of Contents

A Bit About Me 6

Dedication 9

Table of Contents 11

Breads & Muffins 13

Cookies 43

Desserts 65

Miscellaneous 110

Recipes Sorted by Category 145

Recipes Sorted by
   Gluten, Dairy, and Egg Free 147

A Few of My Favourite Things 149

GLUTEN FREE

Breads & Muffins

Biscuits

Gluten & Egg Free

⅔ cup My Favourite GF 1:1 Flour*
¾ tsp. Xanthan Gum
2 tbsps. Cornstarch
1½ tbsps. Baking Powder
¼ tsp. Baking Soda
¼ tsp. Salt
1 tbsp. Sugar
¼ cup Butter, cold
½ cup Milk
½ tsp. Vinegar

*Flour blend is VERY important in end product. If you decide to use a different flour blend, do NOT add the xanthan gum from this recipe if it has a gum already in it, or it will not turn out. You will find my favourite 1:1 flour in this cookbook. If you are using a premade mix, I find Kinnikinnick works the best for premade in my recipes.

Add vinegar to the milk and let it sit while you prepare the biscuits.

In a bowl, measure the flour, xanthan gum, cornstarch, baking powder, baking soda, salt and sugar. With a whisk mix well.

Grate the butter into the dry ingredients. Stir until mixed well. If you try to grate warm butter, it will not work so make sure the butter is cold from the fridge.

Add the milk mixture to the dry ingredients and stir with a

spoon until combined. Cover the dough and place in the fridge for 15 minutes. I did try leaving the chilling step out, and it does make a big difference ... do take the time to chill!

Place chilled dough on a floured pastry mat and roll out to 1-inch thick. Use a 2-inch cookie cutter and cut biscuits out. If you do not have a cookie cutter, my mom always used a glass that was about the right size and it works great!

Place the biscuits onto parchment lined baking sheet.

Bake for 15 minutes in a 400°F oven.

They taste great warm with butter and jam.

Enjoy!

"Behind every recipe you love, is a story you want to share!"

-Family Cookbook Project

Dad's Saturday Morning Waffles

Gluten & Dairy Free

2¾ cups My Favourite 1:1 Gluten Free Flour*
¼ tsp. Salt
½ tsp. Baking Soda
2 tbsps. Sugar
¼ cup Canola Oil
1¾ cup Milk, rice milk if making dairy free
3 Eggs

*Flour blend is VERY important in end product. If you decide to use a different flour blend, do NOT add the xanthan gum from this recipe if it has a gum already in it, or it will not turn out. You will find my favourite 1:1 flour in this cookbook. If you are using a premade mix, I find Kinnikinnick works the best for premade in my recipes.

Measure and mix flour, salt, soda and sugar in a bowl.

In a second bowl, measure and beat the oil, milk and eggs.

Pour liquid mixture into the bowl with the flour mixture. Stir very well. Let sit for 5 minutes.

Turn waffle iron on to heat up. Once it has heated up, then stir the batter again very well. Pour batter into waffle iron and cook as per the waffle iron's instructions.

A Note: My hubby made pancakes since we were first married and then the kids helped him make them as they grew. Once we turned into celiacs, he had to figure out how to keep this tradition.

The gluten free waffles became a new tradition that we all love. It makes Saturday a little more special. Somehow waffles go well with sleepy people, PJ's, and smiles!

Enjoy!

Banana Oatmeal Muffins

Gluten Free

1½ cups My Favourite 1:1 Flour*
1 cup Gluten Free Oats
⅓ cup White Sugar
½ teaspoons Xanthan Gum
1 teaspoons Baking Powder
1 tsp. Cinnamon
1 tsp. Baking Soda
½ tsp. Salt
½ to ⅔ cup Chocolate Chips (optional)
4 Bananas
¼ cup Canola Oil
2 Eggs
¼ cup Skim Milk

*Flour blend is VERY important in end product. If you decide to use a different flour blend, do NOT add the xanthan gum from this recipe if it has a gum already in it, or it will not turn out. You will find my favourite 1:1 flour in this cookbook. If you are using a premade mix, I find Kinnikinnick works the best for premade in my recipes.

In a large bowl measure and mix the dry ingredients and set to the side (do not add the chocolate chips yet).

Get a second bowl and mash the bananas. Add the milk, oil and eggs, mix well. Pour the banana mixture into the dry ingredients and stir with a spoon. Stir a minimum 50 times. This is important! Now add the chocolate chips and stir well.

Scoop dough into prepared muffin tins (either grease or line with papers). You can place 2-3 chocolate chips on top of each muffin before you bake. It makes them look pretty, but not necessary! Let the muffins sit in pan for 15 minutes before you bake them.

Bake in 400°F oven for 20 minutes.

Enjoy!

Garden Apple Muffins

Gluten & Dairy Free

DRY INGREDIENTS
1⅓ cups My Favourite 1:1 Flour*
1 tsp. Xanthan Gum
1½ tsps. Baking Powder
1½ tsps. Baking Soda
½ tsp. Salt
2 tsp. Cinnamon
½ cup White Sugar
¼ cup Brown Sugar

WET INGREDIENTS
¾ cup Applesauce
3 Eggs
1 tsp. Vanilla
2 cups Apples, grated fresh or frozen from my garden

TOPPING
2 tbsps. Raw Sugar
1 tsp. Cinnamon
2 tbsps. Quinoa Flakes
2 tsp. Canola Oil

*Flour blend is VERY important in end product. If you decide to use a different flour blend, do NOT add the xanthan gum from this recipe if it has a gum already in it, or it will not turn out. You will find my favourite 1:1 flour in this cookbook. If you are using a premade mix, I find Kinnikinnick works the best for premade in my recipes.

In a large bowl mix the dry ingredients and in a small bowl mix the wet ingredients. You can leave the peel on your apples or take them off, it is each person's own preference!

Get a second bowl and mix the wet ingredients together.

Pour the wet ingredients into the dry ingredients and stir with a spoon for minimum 50 times. This is important!

Scoop batter into prepared muffin tins (either greased or lined with papers).

Let the muffins sit in pan for 15 minutes before you bake them.

Mix the topping ingredients together and then sprinkle it on top of each muffin.

Bake muffins for 20-25 minutes in a 400°F oven.

A Note: We have two apple trees and I use apples from my tree for this recipe. I grate them up in the fall and measure them out into bags for my freezer so that I can easily make them throughout the winter.

Enjoy!

"Vegetables are a must on a diet. I suggest carrot cake, zucchini bread, and pumpkin pie."
--Jim Davis

Gram's Blueberry Muffins

Gluten Free

DRY INGREDIENTS
1⅓ cups My Favourite 1:1 Flour*
¼ tsps. Xanthan Gum
1 tbsp. Baking Powder
½ tsp. Salt
½ cup White Sugar
1 cup Blueberries, fresh or frozen

WET INGREDIENTS
¼ cup Hard Block Margarine,
   melted (I use Parkay)
1 Egg
¾ cup Skim Milk
1 tsp. Vanilla

TOPPING
2 tbsps. Gluten Free Oats or
   Flaked Quinoa
1 tbsps. Brown Sugar
1 tsp. Cinnamon

*Flour blend is VERY important in end product. If you decide to use a different flour blend, do NOT add the xanthan gum from this recipe if it has a gum already in it, or it will not turn out. You will find my favourite 1:1 flour in this cookbook. If you are using a premade mix, I find Kinnikinnick works the best for premade in my recipes.

In a large bowl mix the dry ingredients and in a small bowl mix the wet ingredients.

Pour the wet ingredients into the dry ingredients and stir with a spoon for minimum 50 times. This is important!

Scoop batter into prepared muffin tins (either greased or lined with papers).

Let the muffins sit in pan for 15 minutes before you bake them.

Mix together the topping ingredients, as you wait. Sprinkle the topping on top of each muffin.

Bake muffins for 20-25 minutes in a 400°F oven.

A Note: These muffins scream YOU ARE HOME to me! My gramma and mom made these all of the time growing up. The smell and taste make me feel like I am home.

I am so glad that I figured out how to make them gluten free style!

Enjoy!

> *"Nothing would be more tiresome than eating and drinking if God had not made them a pleasure as well as a necessity."*
> *--Voltaire*

Lemon Poppyseed Muffins

Gluten Free

DRY INGREDIENTS
2 cups My Favourite 1:1 Flour*
½ cup Sugar
1 tsp. Xanthan Gum
1/2 tsp. Baking Soda
1 tbsp. Baking Powder
1/2 tsp. Salt
3 tbsps. Poppyseeds
1 tbsp. Lemon Zest

WET INGREDIENTS
2 Eggs
½ cup Canola Oil
¼ cup Milk
¼ cup Cream
½ tsp. Vanilla
7 tbsps. Fresh Lemon Juice

GLAZE:
½ cup Icing Sugar
3 tbsps. Fresh Lemon Juice

*Flour blend is VERY important in end product. If you decide to use a different flour blend, do NOT add the xanthan gum from this recipe if it has a gum already in it, or it will not turn out. You will find my favourite 1:1 flour in this cookbook. If you are using a premade mix, I find Kinnikinnick works the best for premade in my recipes.

In a Kitchen-aid mixing bowl add the dry ingredients. Mix gently with paddle.

In a small bowl mix the eggs, oil, milk, cream, vanilla and lemon juice.

Pour the wet ingredients slowly into the dry ingredients. Mix for 2 minutes on low speed. Scoop into 12 muffins greased or lined muffin cups. Let sit for 10 minutes before you bake.

Bake for 20 minutes in a 350°F oven.

Mix the glaze ingredients in a bowl until smooth, while you wait for the muffins to bake, set to the side.

Once muffins come out of oven, use a skewer to poke many holes into each muffin. Then, use a spoon to pour the lemon glaze over the top of each muffin. Let the muffins sit in the pan for 10 minutes and then take out and leave on cooling rack to cool.

A Note: My family LOVES these muffins.

Some gluten free baking is very gummy when it is warm from the oven, yet these muffins are not and taste good while they are still warm!

Enjoy!

"Do vegetarians eat animal crackers?"
--Unknown

Healthy Banana Loaf

Gluten & Dairy Free with Egg Free option

DRY INGREDIENTS
¾ cup Garbanzo or Chickpea Flour
¾ cup Brown Rice Flour
1 tsp. Xanthan Gum
2 tsp. Baking Powder
¼ tsp. Baking Soda
½ tsp. Salt
1 tbsp. Chia Seed, whole
1½ tsp. Cinnamon
½ cup Pecans, chopped
½ cup Chocolate Chips

WET INGREDIENTS
½ cup Honey
½ cup Canola Oil
1 tsp. Vanilla
4 Bananas
2 Eggs (or you can substitute with 2 flax eggs. Measure and let sit, 2 tbsps. Flax Meal with 4 tbsps. warm water). If you can eat eggs, it turns out the best with eggs.

In a large bowl measure the dry ingredients, blend well and then set to the side.

Get a second bowl and mash the bananas. Add the wet ingredients. Mix well.

Pour the banana mixture into the dry ingredients and stir with a spoon. Stir minimum 50 times. This is important!

Scoop dough into prepared loaf or muffin tins (either grease or line with papers).

Bake in 350°F oven.

Loaf 50-55 minutes.

Muffins 20 - 25 minutes.

The top of the loaf will be brown, and it can look like it is done but the inside of loaf can be doughy.

To check if it is fully cooked, place a knife down the middle of the loaf to ensure the knife comes out without any dough stuck to it. If dough is on knife, then put loaf back into oven until it is done.

A Note: My celiac son absolutely LOVES these muffins.

He would eat them every morning for breakfast if they were available.

Enjoy!

"Laughter is brightest in the place where food is."
--Irish Proverb

Pumpkin Date Muffins

Gluten & Dairy Free

2 cups My Favourite GF BROWN Flour, in this book
½ cup Brown Sugar
¼ cup White Sugar
2 tsps. Baking Soda
1 tsp. Baking Powder
¾ tsp. Xanthan Gum
1½ tsps. Cinnamon
¼ tsp. Nutmeg
¼ tsp. Cloves
½ tsp. Salt
1 cup Pumpkin, pureed
½ cup Canola Oil
½ cup Boiling Water
2 Eggs
¾ cup Dates

TOPPING
2 tablespoons Quinoa Flakes
2 tablespoons Cane Sugar
1 teaspoon Cinnamon

Chop dates and place in bowl with boiling water, set to the side to cool. Measure Baking Soda and stir into the date mixture.

In a large bowl mix all the other dry ingredients.

In a small bowl mix the pumpkin, oil and eggs.

Pour all the ingredients together and stir 50 times.

Scoop dough into prepared muffin tins (either greased or lined with papers).

Let the muffins sit in prepared tins for 10 minutes.

Mix the topping and then sprinkle it onto the muffins.

Bake muffins for approximately 20 minutes in 350ºF oven.

Enjoy!

Raspberry Muffins

Gluten Free

DRY INGREDIENTS
1⅓ cups My Favourite 1:1 GF All Purpose Flour*
¼ tsp. Xanthan Gum
1 tbsp. Baking Powder
½ tsp. Salt
½ cup White Sugar
1 cup Raspberries, fresh or frozen

WET INGREDIENTS
¼ cup Hard Block Margarine, melted (I use Parkay)
1 Egg
¾ cup Skim Milk
½ tsp. Almond Extract

TOPPING
2 tbsps. Raw Sugar
½ tsp. Cinnamon

*Flour blend is VERY important in end product. If you decide to use a different flour blend, do NOT add the xanthan gum from this recipe if it has a gum already in it, or it will not turn out. You will find my favourite 1:1 flour in this cookbook. If you are using a premade mix, I find Kinnikinnick works the best for premade in my recipes.

In a large bowl mix the dry ingredients and in a small bowl mix the wet ingredients. Pour the wet ingredients into the dry and stir with a spoon for minimum 50 times.

Scoop batter into prepared muffin tins (either greased or lined with papers). Let the muffins sit in pan for 15 minutes before you bake them.

Mix the topping ingredients together and then sprinkle it on top of each muffin. Bake muffins for 20-25 minutes in a 400°F oven.

Enjoy!

Mini Cornbread Loaves

Gluten Free

¾ cup White Rice Flour
¼ cup Brown Rice Flour
½ cup Quinoa Flour
1½ cups Cornmeal, make sure certified gluten free
¼ cup Sugar
1 tbsp. Baking Powder
½ tsp. Baking Soda
2½ cups Milk
1 tsp. Vinegar
3 Eggs, room temperature
⅓ cup Butter, melted and cooled

In a large bowl mix the dry ingredients and in a small bowl mix the wet ingredients.

Pour the wet ingredients into the dry ingredients and stir with a spoon until well mixed, and then mix a little longer!

Scoop the batter into a greased mini loaf pan. I have a mini loaf pan that takes two muffin scoops of batter per mini loaf. Let sit for 10 minutes before baking.

Bake for 20 minutes in a 400°F oven.

Serve warm from the oven. They are not gummy if you eat warm, they taste the best warm from the oven with something like a bowl of chili on the side.

A Note: Our family loves to cut them in half, put some butter on and then a smidge of Rogers Golden Syrup.

When I grew up my dad would put Rogers Golden Syrup on biscuits .... So, I passed this on to my kids with the corn bread. Definitely a Grandpa thing!

Enjoy!

FlatBread

Gluten, Dairy & Egg Free

1½ cups Warm Water
½ tsp. Salt
1 tsp. Garlic Powder
100 grams Coconut Flour
55 grams Tapioca Starch, make sure to NOT use Tapioca FLOUR
3 tbsps. Psyllium Husk, whole not powdered
Oil
Course Salt

In your Kitchen-aid bowl, measure and stir the salt, garlic powder, coconut flour and tapioca starch.

In a measuring cup add the water and then psyllium husk, stir. Pour into the dry ingredients and mix with paddle attachment until well combined.

I use my scale to weigh the entire 'lump' of dough. Then I divide it into 12-15 sections, using the scale. You can divide into any amount that you wish ... the flat bread will be smaller or bigger depending on what you choose.

Dust a pastry mat with some tapioca starch and then start rolling out your divided 'lumps' of dough. I have used a Tortilla press to flatten each lump. Yet, I find using a rolling pin faster and easier ... I do not care if each piece is an exact circle. You do want them to be fairly thin like a tortilla. The dough is not sticky and is easy to roll out.

Heat your non-stick griddle to 300°F.

Cook your flat bread for 1 to 2 minutes per side. When I flip the flat bread on the griddle, I use a pastry brush to lightly brush oil on the cooked side and sprinkle some course salt.

Repeat until all of the 'lumps' have been cooked.

A Note: I make these when we are eating Butter Chicken or something like that.

I cook and serve them up hot while we are eating, and the kids love it!

The flat bread does not break, and it tastes great. You can eat it on the side with any dish or wrap your butter chicken inside of it like the photo.

Enjoy!

"I would like to find a stew that will give me heartburn immediately, instead of at three o'clock in the morning."
--John Barrymore

Bagels

Gluten Free

5 cups My Favourite GF 1:1 Flour*
2 tsps. Xanthan Gum
¼ cup Milk Powder
2 tbsps. Whole Psyllium Husk, not powdered
2 tsps. Baking Powder
2 tsps. Salt
2 tbsps. Brown Sugar
1 tbsp. Instant Yeast
2 tbsps. Butter, melted
2 tsps. Apple Cider Vinegar
2¼ cups Warm Water, 95-100°F
2 Egg Whites
¾ cup Fresh Blueberries, cut in half

ITEMS NEEDED FOR COOKING
½ cup Sugar, used when boiling
2 cups Ice Cubes
1 tsp. Baking Soda
2 tbsps. Sugar
Water

*Flour blend is VERY important in end product. If you decide to use a different flour blend, do NOT add the xanthan gum from this recipe if it has a gum already in it, or it will not turn out. You will find my favourite 1:1 flour in this cookbook. If you are using a premade mix, I find Kinnikinnick works the best for premade in my recipes.

Add flour, xanthan gum, baking powder, salt, brown sugar and psyllium husk to your mixing bowl and mix for a few seconds with the paddle attachment. Then add the milk powder and yeast, mix again.

Then add butter, apple cider vinegar, warm water and egg whites. Beat for 3 minutes. Cover and let rise for 1 hour, or when it has approximately doubled in size. If your house is warm it could rise as quickly as 30 minutes and if it's cooler it will take the hour.

Stir in blueberries or any flavour of your choice (ideas are cinnamon raisin, cheese or just leave plain). Stir on low with paddle attachment until just mixed in. If you are leaving plain, still mix for a few seconds.

Divide dough into 10 equal pieces, I use my large scoop (each bagel gets 2 scoops). Shape each lump of dough into a circle/disc and then use your fingers to push a hole in the centre to make it look like a bagel and then place on a parchment lined baking pan. The dough is sticky and not the easiest to work with. Get a cup of water and dip your fingers in once in a while to make your fingers less sticky with the dough! Once all 10 bagels are on your lined baking pan, place the baking pan into the freezer for 2-3 hours.

You can then take the frozen bagels out of freezer and wrap each bagel in wax paper and then put them into a container or a freezer bag and freeze until you want to make bagels in the future. You can make 1 or 2 bagels any day that you want them and leave the rest frozen. You've done all the work ahead of time and all you have to do now is cook them as you want them. It's pretty amazing to have fresh bagels!

Turn the oven on to 500°F and place a metal cake pan on the bottom rack of your oven.

Add 10 cups of water and 1/2 cup sugar to a large pot and bring to a boil. Use a spoon to make sure the sugar is dissolved and mixed.

Now bring your bagels out of the freezer. You are ready to boil your frozen bagels. Just before you boil, put 1 teaspoon of baking soda in the water. Put 2 to 3 bagels in the water UPSIDE DOWN and set your timer for 1 minute. Flip the bagels and set your timer for an additional 1 minute. Use a slotted spoon and take your bagels out of the water and place them on a cooling rack (that has a tray underneath to catch the drips). Once they have dripped off the extra water, place onto a parchment lined baking pan.

Fill a 2-cup measuring cup with ice & then very cold water to the 2-cup line, pour the water and ice into the cake pan that is already hot in the oven and close the oven door quickly, as you want to keep all of the steam in the oven.

Mix 2 tablespoons of water and sugar in a bowl and then use a pastry brush to 'paint' the sugar water onto the bagels. Place the bagels into the oven quickly and shut the door, trying to keep the steam in the oven. Immediately turn down the oven to 450°F. Set the timer for 15 minutes. Once the time is up, turn your oven off and let the bagels sit in the oven for 5 minutes without opening the door.

It's hard to know if they are cooked, as they will brown on the outside and could be doughy on the inside. So, if you have a digital thermometer, take its temperature! If it is 200°F it is cooked. Then cool for 15 minutes before you eat.

These have a crispy outside and chewy inside, like a bagel should be!

Enjoy!

"Man shall not live on bread alone."
--Matthew 4:4

Baguettes

Gluten, Dairy & Egg Free

2 cups Warm Water, 110°F
1 tbsp. Instant Yeast
½ tbsp. Maple Syrup
½ tbsp. Honey
2 tbsp. Olive Oil
2 cups Brown Rice Flour
¾ cup Tapioca Starch
1 tsp. Italian Seasoning
½ tsp. Garlic Powder
1 tsp. Salt
¼ cup White Chia, ground not whole
¼ cup Flax Meal
¼ cup Whole Psyllium Husk, not powdered
1 tbsp. Olive Oil, for brushing
Course Salt, to sprinkle on top of baguette

In a measuring cup take the temperature of the water and make sure it is close to 110°F. Then, add maple syrup, honey, oil & yeast, stir gently. Set to the side while you gather other ingredients.

In a Kitchen-aid mixing bowl add your rice flour, tapioca starch, spices, and salt. Mix.

Add the chia, flax & psyllium husk to the water mixture & stir. Let sit for 60 seconds (no more or it will go solid…Trust me!) & then stir again. Quickly, pour the chia water mixture into the flour mixture & beat with a Kitchen-aid paddle for 3 MINUTES. Set your timer!

Preheat oven to 400°F.

Cut the dough in half (I weigh the dough). Put the dough onto a very lightly floured pastry mat and shape each baguette with lightly floured hands. This dough is very easy to work with and shape. Each baguette should be 12" long.

Place the shaped baguettes onto parchment lined baking sheet.

With a pastry brush, brush lightly with olive oil and sprinkle with course sea salt on top. The oil makes the baguette brown nicely and the salt makes it look pretty, it is optional. Then, I use a sharp knife and cut a few shallow lines into the top of the baguettes to make it look 'fancy'. Let the dough sit for 30 minutes to rise.

Bake in a preheated oven for 35 to 40 minutes. Cool completely before serving. If you do not let it cool, it will be gummy. We like ours dipped in olive oil & balsamic vinegar. You can warm it up after it cools and it is not gummy.

Enjoy!

"One who is full loathes honey from the comb, but to the hungry even what is bitter tastes sweet."

--Proverbs 27:

Mom's Loaf

Gluten, Dairy & Egg Free

Flax Egg (1 tbsp. Flax Meal & 3 tbsps. Warm Water)
2½ cups Warm Water (110 F)
1 tbsp. Instant Yeast
2 tbsps. Maple Syrup
2 tbsps. Olive Oil
1 tbsp. Molasses
⅓ cup Chia Seeds, ground (I grind in my magic bullet)
⅓ cup Psyllium Husk, whole not powdered
162 grams Sorghum Flour
172 grams Millet Flour
92 grams Buckwheat Flour
43 grams Teff Flour
180 grams Brown Rice Flour
34 grams Amaranth Flour
1 tsp. Salt
2 tsps. Cinnamon
¼ cup Dried Apricots
¼ cup Dried Craisins
¼ cup Raisins

Make your flax egg and let it sit in a bowl until you need it.

In a large measuring cup add the water, maple syrup, honey, oil, molasses and yeast. Stir gently and let sit for 5 minutes.

After 5 minutes, add the chia and psyllium husk. It's important to STIR the chia and psyllium husk in QUICKLY or it will clump. Then let the mixture sit for 60 seconds and stir again. Do not let it sit any longer or it will become SOLID (I know from experience!).

Add chia mixture and flax egg to the dry ingredients and mix in your Kitchen-aid on the low setting for 10 seconds. Then 1 minute on medium setting. On the low setting, mix in the dried fruit.

On a lightly floured pastry mat, knead dough ... adding a

bit of gluten free brown rice flour at a time. You are kneading and adding a bit of flour to get a non-sticky dough. Once you've reached a bread dough texture that is not Sticky and easy to handle, stop adding flour. It will not take much flour to get this consistency, maybe a tablespoon or two.

You can now make the dough into a loaf shape. You can bake it in a greased loaf pan ... or shape it into an artisan loaf and place it on a parchment lined baking sheet

Brush loaf with oil and sprinkle with chia, buckwheat or flax on top (this is to make it look nice). Then use a sharp knife to make tiny shallow cuts on top of the loaf to add to the artisan look.

Let the loaf sit for 45 minutes to 1 hour to rise. Then place the loaf in a 400°F oven for 55-60 minutes.

Cool pan on cooling rack for 15 minutes and then remove pan and allow loaf to cool on a cooling rack.

Slice, put parchment between slices, place in a container or freezer bag and enjoy one piece at a time.

A Note: This bread does not taste good warm from the oven. If the lovely bread smell gets to you and you think you will try a piece warm from the oven, it will be gummy and does not cut or taste nice.

Once it has cooled completely, it tastes fabulous! It is my favourite bread for breakfast. I toast it and then put a pit of butter and it really has a lovely taste.

This loaf is FULL of nutrients, iron, and fibre. It will stick to your ribs

and nourish you ... what a great way to start a day!

Enjoy!

"Good bread is the most fundamentally satisfying of all foods; good bread with fresh butter, the greatest of feasts!"
--James Beard

Cinnamon Buns

Gluten, Dairy & Egg Free

1½ cups Brown Rice Flour
½ cup White Rice Flour
½ cup Tapioca Starch
¼ cup Potato Starch
½ tsp. Salt
1 tsp. Baking Powder
1 Flax Egg (1 tbsp. ground flax & 2 tbsps. water)
1 tbsp. Instant Yeast
½ tbsp. Honey
½ tbsp. Maple Syrup
2 tbsps. Olive Oil
2 cups Warm Water
½ cup Ground Chia
¼ cup WHOLE Psyllium Husk
¼ cup Butter or Coconut Oil (if dairy free)
½ cup Brown Sugar
3 tbsps. Cinnamon

GLAZE
1 cup Icing Sugar
2 to 3 tbsps. Milk of Choice

In a small dish, combine the "flax egg" (water and ground flax) and set to the side. Or you can use an egg if you choose.

In your mixing bowl place, warm water, yeast, maple syrup and honey. Stir gently and let it sit.

In a separate bowl stir your flours, starches, salt, and baking powder. Set to the side.

Add your oil, flax egg, ground chia and psyllium husk to the water mixture, stir quickly to combine. Let it sit for 1 minute and stir again. Pour the dry ingredients into the mixing bowl with the water mixture. Mix on low until combined and then increase the speed to medium. Mix for 3 minutes.

Roll out the dough into a rectangle that is approximately

12"x16" in size. You can use a bit of brown rice flour if the dough is a bit sticky, but you won't need much. Pour melted butter or coconut oil evenly onto the dough, then evenly spread the brown sugar and cinnamon on top.

Roll the dough into a 'log' and cut into pieces, about 1-inch each. Separate the pieces you have cut, and you will have circles. Place the circles into a greased pie plate. If you have extra, bake them in a muffin tin.

Let the plate of cinnamon buns rise for 25 minutes.

Bake at 400°F for 20-25 minutes.

Mix the glaze together in a small bowl. Drizzle glaze over the warm cinnamon buns.

Buns taste great warm!

A Note: These are tasty!

They have great texture and are the best cinnamon buns that I have eaten since being diagnosed celiac.

Waking up any morning to warm cinnamon buns is a nice treat.

Enjoy!

"One of the very nicest things about life is the way we must regularly stop whatever it is we are doing and devote our attention to eating."
--Luciano Pavarott

GLUTEN FREE

Cookies

Chocolate Chip Cookies

Gluten & Dairy Free

1 cup HardBlock Margarine, I use Parkay
1 cup Sugar
½ cup Brown Sugar
2 Eggs
2 tsps. Vanilla
1 tsp. Baking Soda
1 tsp. Xanthan Gum
½ tsp. Salt
½ tsp. Cinnamon
2 cups My Favourite 1:1 Flour*
2 cups Chocolate Chips
1 cup Pecans, chopped (optional)

*Flour blend is VERY important in end product. If you decide to use a different flour blend, do NOT add the xanthan gum from this recipe if it has a gum already in it, or it will not turn out. You will find my favourite 1:1 flour in this cookbook. If you are using a premade mix, I find Kinnikinnick works the best for premade in my recipes.

Mix the margarine and sugars in the Kitchen-aid.

Add one egg at a time and then vanilla. Scrape sides of bowl. Then add dry ingredients until mixed well.

Add chocolate chips and pecans (if using) and mix until well combined.

Drop with tablespoon scoop onto parchment lined baking sheets. Flatten with the palm of hand or with a fork.

Bake for 8-10 minutes in a 375°F oven.

Take out of oven when edges of cookies are just starting to brown. Leave pan on cooking rack for 15 minutes. Transfer, with flipper, to cooling rack.

A Note: I usually only cook one pan of cookies.

Then I freeze a baking sheet full of flattened cookie dough cookies (cookie frozen pucks). Once frozen I put cookie pucks into a freezer bag and then I have cookies to bake fresh at any time.

Enjoy!

"Go, eat your food with gladness."
--Ecclesiastes 9:7

Birds Nest Cookies

Gluten & Dairy Free

½ cup HardBlock Margarine, I use Parkay
¼ cup Sugar
1 Egg, separated
½ tsp. Almond Extract
1 cup My Favourite Gluten Free 1:1 Flour*
1 tsp. Xanthan Gum
¾ cup Pecans or Walnuts, finely chopped
Jam or Jelly of your choice. I normally use raspberry jam.

*Flour blend is VERY important in end product. If you decide to use a different flour blend, do NOT add the xanthan gum from this recipe if it has a gum already in it, or it will not turn out. You will find my favourite 1:1 flour in this cookbook. If you are using a premade mix, I find Kinnikinnick works the best for premade in my recipes.

Cream butter/margarine and sugar until smooth. Then add egg yolk and almond extract, beat until well mixed.

Add the gluten free flour and xanthan gum.

Mix the dough well once you have added the flour and xanthan gum.

Roll dough into 3/4" balls and place onto a plate.

Then put the egg white into a bowl and beat with a fork, set to the side.

In a second bowl place the chopped nuts, set to the side.

Take balls of dough and roll them in egg and then nuts. Ensure they are evenly covered. This is a messy endeavor, so you may need to wash your hands a few times while doing this!

Place nut covered cookies onto parchment lined baking sheets.

Make an indent in the middle of each cookie with your thumb or a wooden spoon handle.

Bake cookies in a 350°F oven for 5 minutes. Then take the sheet of cookies out and push down the indent again with your thumb or wooden spoon handle. Work fast!

Bake for an additional 5-7 minutes, or until the bottoms are golden.

Cool these cookies on the baking sheet and do not attempt to move them to a cooling rack until they are **completely** cooled, or they will crumble!

Fill cookies with jam/jelly while the cookies are still hot on the pan.

These cookies also free well and taste great.

Enjoy!

"The belly rules the mind."
--Spanish Proverb

Chewy Gingersnap Cookies

Gluten & Dairy Free

½ cup Canola Oil
1 cup Sugar
¼ cup Molasses
1 Egg
1 tsp. Vanilla
1 ¾ cups My Favourite 1:1 GF All Purpose Flour*
2 tsps. Ginger
1 tsp. Cinnamon
1 tsp. Baking Powder
½ tsp. Xanthan Gum*
1 tsp. Baking Soda
½ tsp. Salt

*Flour blend is VERY important in end product. If you decide to use a different flour blend, do NOT add the xanthan gum from this recipe if it has a gum already in it, or it will not turn out. You will find my favourite 1:1 flour in this cookbook. If you are using a premade mix, I find Kinnikinnick works the best for premade in my recipes.

With your Kitchen-Aid or electric mixer, mix the canola oil, sugar, molasses, vanilla, and egg.

In a separate bowl measure and whisk the gluten free flour blend, ginger, cinnamon, baking powder, xanthan gum, baking soda, and salt. Then add it to your wet ingredients and mix well. Place a few tablespoons of white sugar on a plate.

I use a 1 tablespoon scoop to measure the dough, and then roll it into a ball. Then dip the top of the ball of dough in the sugar. Place the ball on a parchment lined baking sheet (with the sugar facing up). Flatten with the palm of your hands.

Bake for 8 minutes in a 375°F oven. You will know they are done when cracks JUST start to form on the top of the cookie.

If you leave the cookies in the oven longer, they will be a very hard gingersnap. Let the baking sheet of cookies cool on a rack before transferring them, or they will fall apart.

A Note: My mother-in-law made these scrumptious ginger cookies whenever we came to visit the farm. They are chewy and soft and smell just like Christmas.

She made them all year, luckily for us we didn't have to wait to have them at Christmas! Our family enjoys them and thinks of her whenever I make them in our home … gluten free style!

Enjoy,
Teresa

"When baking, follow directions. When cooking, go by your own taste."
--Laiko Bahrs

Dan's Cookies

Gluten & Dairy Free

1 cup Hard Block Margarine, I use Parkay
1 cup Brown Sugar
2 Eggs
1 tsp. Vanilla
1¾ cups My Favourite GF All Purpose Flour*
½ tsp. Baking Soda
1 tsp. Baking Powder
¾ tsp. Xanthan Gum
½ tsp. Salt
1 tsp. Cinnamon
⅔ cup Gluten Free Oats
⅔ cup Gluten Free Rice Krispies
⅓ cup Coconut
1 cup Chocolate Chips
¾ cup Pecans, chopped

*Flour blend is VERY important in end product. If you decide to use a different flour blend, do NOT add the xanthan gum from this recipe if it has a gum already in it, or it will not turn out. You will find my favourite 1:1 flour in this cookbook. If you are using a premade mix, I find Kinnikinnick works the best for premade in my recipes.

Mix the margarine and sugar in the Kitchen-aid. Add one egg at a time, and then the vanilla.

In a separate bowl, measure flour, oats, xanthan gum, baking powder, soda, salt, and cinnamon. Add these dry ingredients to the butter mixture and beat until well combined. Scrape bowl. Add rice krispies, chocolate chips, coconut and nuts until just combined, do not over mix.

Drop by tablespoon scoop onto parchment lined baking sheets. Flatten each cookie with a fork.

Bake for 10 minutes, or until golden around sides, in a 350°F oven. Leave pan on cooling rack for 15 minutes. Then transfer cookies, with flipper, to cooling rack.

Enjoy

Hubby's Monster Cookies

Gluten & Dairy Free

195 grams White Sugar
215 grams Brown Sugar
½ cup Hard Block Margarine, I use Parkay
3 Eggs
355 grams Peanut Butter
1 tsp. Vanilla
4½ cups Gluten Free Oats
2 tsps. Baking Soda
1 cup M&M's
½ cup Chocolate Chips

Place all the above ingredients into your Kitchen-aid mixing bowl and mix until well combined.

I place my bowl on my digital kitchen scale and just pour and scoop the ingredients in while I weigh each ingredient. It's much easier to weigh peanut butter straight into your bowl than to use measuring cups! Less waste and mess.

Use the 2-tablespoon size of scoop to measure dough onto parchment lined baking sheets.

Flatten each cookie with the palm of your hand.

I take one new M&M and make sure one is on top of each cookie, this is only for visual appeal once cooked.

Bake for 12 minutes in a 350°F oven.

You will know they are done when they get a bit brown on the edges and don't look doughy. If you over bake, they will be crispy cookies, I like them chewy instead!

I usually only cook one pan of cookies. Then I freeze a baking pan of flattened cookie dough cookies (cookie pucks). Once frozen I put cookie pucks into a freezer bag and you can have cookies to bake fresh at any time.

A Note: My mom made monster cookies when I was young and I loved them back then and my family, especially Hubby, loves these cookies!

It is neat that these cookies do not have any flour. If you have intolerances to potatoes or other starches, this is a good alternative.

Gluten Free Oats can make some celiacs sick, therefore I have tried making these cookies with quinoa flakes, but it does not turn out.

These freeze well and defrost quickly.

Enjoy!

"A balanced diet is a cookie in each hand
--Barbara Johnson

Flourless Peanut Butter Cookies

Gluten & Dairy Free

440 grams Smooth Peanut Butter
½ cup White Sugar
½ cup Brown Sugar
1 Egg
1 tsp. Baking Powder
1 tsp. Baking Soda
1 tsp. Vanilla

Measure all the ingredients into your Kitchen-aid mixing bowl and mix well.

Scoop the dough into 1 tablespoon balls. Pick up each ball of dough and roll into a ball with palm of hands and then place onto parchment lined baking sheets. Flatten cookies using a fork that has been dipped in water. Press fork one direction on top of cookie and then the opposite on each cookie.

Bake in a 350°F oven for 10 minutes.

A Note: My neighbour made these for us when my son was first diagnosed. It was such a loving and encouraging thing for her to do for him. It meant so much. Thank you, 'my neighbour', for the recipe and bring some joy during that time!

These are one of our daughters' favourite cookies … she thinks they are better than *any* peanut butter cookie she has met!

"No man in the world has more courage than the man who can stop after eating one peanut."
--Channing Pollock

Chocolate Sandwich Cookies

Gluten & Egg Free

COOKIE INGREDIENTS
1 ¼ cup My Favourite 1:1 Flour*
1 tsp. Xanthan Gum
¾ cup Sugar
1/4 tsp. Baking Soda
1/2 tsp. Salt
1 tsp. Instant Coffee
10 tbsps. Cocoa
4 tbsps. Milk
1 tbsp. Cream
1 tsp. Vanilla
½ cup Hard Block Margarine, I use Parkay
¼ cup Butter

FILLNG INGREDIENTS
1⅓ cup White Chocolate
⅓ cup Cream
2 tbsps. Icing Sugar
5 drops Food Coloring, if you want the filling to be a color other than white

*Flour blend is VERY important in end product. If you decide to use a different flour blend, do NOT add the xanthan gum from this recipe if it has a gum already in it, or it will not turn out. You will find my favourite 1:1 flour in this cookbook. If you are using a premade mix, I find Kinnikinnick works the best for premade in my recipes.

Place the flour, cocoa, sugar, baking soda, salt, xanthan gum, and instant coffee into your Kitchen-Aid mixing bowl and use a whisk to mix the ingredients.

Cut up your butter and margarine and place it into your dry ingredients. Use your paddle attachment and mix on low for 1 minute. Then add the vanilla, cream and milk and mix until it is a soft dough. Divide the dough in half. Use your hands to shape each piece of dough into a round ball.

Place a piece of wax paper on pastry mat and then place one round ball of dough on top of the wax paper. Then place a second piece of wax paper on top of your dough. Roll out the dough to ¼ inch thick.

Placed the rolled dough, still between the wax paper, then into the fridge. Repeat steps with the second ball of dough. Chill for 30 minutes.

Remove one piece of dough from the fridge, leaving the wax paper on, and place it on top of your pastry mat. Gently pull off the top piece of wax paper.

Use a shamrock cookie cutter (or any shape!) and cut out as many as you can. Let your imagination make something fun!

Place the cut-out cookies on to a parchment lined baking sheet.

Bake in a 350°F oven for 10 minutes. Remove from oven and place baking sheet on cooling rack for 10 minutes. Then transfer cookies to cooling rack to cool completely.

FILLING

Place white chocolate in a bowl. In another small bowl, heat the cream in a microwave for 30 seconds. Pour the cream onto the white chocolate and let it sit. If you are using food coloring add it to the melted chocolate and stir. Add the icing sugar and stir. You can add more cream or icing sugar if you need to adjust the texture. It will thicken as it cools.

Put the filling into a ziploc bag. Cut a small corner out of the bag and gently squeeze the filling onto the bottom cookie and then line up another cookie and place on top of filling, gently press together.

These cookies are great, as this filling does not make the cookies soft or mushy. You can put all the icing in and have them made ahead, or let your kids have fun and do their own. You can also put as much or as little filling that you like!

Enjoy!

Spice Cookies

Gluten, Dairy & Egg Free

1 tbsp. Flax Meal
3 tbsp. Warm Water

FIRST SET of INGREDIENTS
1 cup Millet
1 cup Buckwheat (make sure certified GF as buckwheat can easily be cross contaminated in the milling process)
¼ cup Gluten Free Oat Flour
1 tsp. Xanthan Gum
1 tsp. Baking Soda
1 tsp. Dry Ginger
2 tsps. Cinnamon
¼ tsp. Nutmeg

SECOND SET of INGREDIENTS
⅓ cup Olive Oil
⅓ cup Canola Oil
⅓ cup Molasses
1 cup Brown Sugar

In a bowl mix all of the 1st SET of INGREDIENTS, and then set to the side.

Place the 2nd SET of INGREDIENTS in your Kitchen-aid bowl. Mix well.

Add the flax egg and 1st set of ingredients to the kitchen-aid ingredients and mix well.

Place the bowl of dough in the freezer for 15 minutes.

Then use your 1 tablespoon scoop to scoop cookie dough onto parchment lined cookie sheets.

Flatten each lump of cookie dough with the palm of your hand.

Then sprinkle with raw sugar (optional, just makes it look nice!).

Bake for 10-12 minutes in a 350°F oven.

Let cool on pan without touching for 15 minutes.

A Note: The nice thing about these cookies is that they have nutrients and fibre ... PLUS ... they are free from gluten, dairy and egg ... plus they taste great!

Enjoy!

"Chili represents your three stages of matter: solid, liquid, and eventually gas."
--John Goodman as Dan Conner

Sugar Cookies

Gluten & Dairy Free

2½ cups My Favourite 1:1 GF All Purpose Flour*
⅔ cups Sugar
½ tsp. Xanthan Gum*
½ tsp. Salt
1 tsp. Vanilla
2 Eggs
1 cup Hard Block Margarine, I use Parkay

*Flour blend is VERY important in end product. If you decide to use a different flour blend, do NOT add the xanthan gum from this recipe if it has a gum already in it, or it will not turn out. You will find my favourite 1:1 flour in this cookbook. If you are using a premade mix, I find Kinnikinnick works the best for premade in my recipes.

In a bowl, whisk the flour, salt, and xanthan gum. Set to the side.

With an electric mixer, beat the softened margarine and sugar until creamed.

Beat in the eggs and vanilla.

Slowly add the dry ingredients. Beat the dough until it is well combined and sticks together.

On a lightly floured pastry mat, roll out small portions of dough at a time. I use a handy rolling pin that has rings on the end that allows me to roll dough evenly, I find it works well. With a highly floured cookie cutter, cut dough into desired shapes. Be gentle transferring shapes to a parchment lined baking sheet.

Bake for eight minutes in a 350° F oven. You will know the cookies are done when the edges are just turning golden.

Let the cookies cool completely on sheets, or they will crumble.

Transfer to a cooling rack and then decorate when you are ready.

These cookies freeze well. I often make them ahead and then bring them out to decorate when I have time. The decorated cookies can be put back into the freezer and then taken out when needed.

I like to decorate sugar cookies with royal icing, you will find that recipe in this book.

A Note: I have made sugar cookies since our kids were little.

Sugar cookies really are a hit round our house for any occasion. I have hundreds of cookie cutters and love making them. It is one of my favourite things to make!

Enjoy,
Teresa

"A nickel will get you on the subway, but garlic will get you a seat."
--Old New York Proverb

Royal Icing for Sugar Cookies

Gluten & Dairy Free

1 bag (1kg). Icing Sugar
5 tbsps. Meringue Powder*
¾ cup Warm Water
2 tsps. Vanilla Extract

*Meringue Powder can be hard to find gluten free. I have found some online or in my local Bulk Barn (sealed bag).

Stir the icing sugar and meringue powder in a mixing bowl.

In a glass measuring cup stir the flavour into the warm water.

Turn the Kitchen-Aid or electric mixer on the lowest setting and slowly add the water mixture to the icing sugar mixture. The icing will become thick. Continue to add the water until it becomes a honey consistency. Then stop adding water and mix on medium speed for 2 minutes. The icing will become thick and fluffy.

When you are piping around the edge of a cookie, the icing should be the consistency of toothpaste. The flooding consistency should be like liquid hand soap. Just add a 1/4 teaspoon of water at a time to reach proper consistency. It doesn't take much water to change how thick the icing is, so add water slowly!

You can put icing into sandwich or decorating bags to decorate the cookies. It makes it easy to decorate with less mess!

Enjoy!

Snickerdoodle Cookies

Gluten & Dairy Free

1 cup Hard Block Margarine, I use Parkay
1 cup Sugar
2 Eggs
2 tsps. Vanilla
1 tsp. Baking Soda
2 tsps. Xanthan Gum
½ tsp. Salt
2 tsps. Cream of Tartar
3¼ cups My Favourite GF 1:1 Flour*

COATING
¼ cup White Sugar
2 tbsps. Cinnamon

*Flour blend is VERY important in end product. If you decide to use a different flour blend, do NOT add the xanthan gum from this recipe if it has a gum already in it, or it will not turn out. You will find my favourite 1:1 flour in this cookbook. If you are using a premade mix, I find Kinnikinnick works the best for premade in my recipes.

In a ziploc bag measure the coating ingredients, shake, and then set to the side.

Beat together the margarine and sugar in a Kitchen-aid. Scrape the sides and add the vanilla and eggs. Mix well.

In a separate bowl stir together the baking soda, xanthan gum, salt, cream of tartar and flour.

Add the dry ingredients to the wet and mix thoroughly.

Use a tablespoon scoop to form balls of dough. Roll balls with your hands to make a perfect circle. Then, place a few balls at a time into your sealed sugar ziploc bag and shake gently to coat.

Place sugar coated cookies onto a parchment lined baking sheet. Use your hand to flatten the cookie.

Bake for 8 minutes in a 375°F oven.

They will stay soft if you do not overcook! Cook until little cracks start to form on the side of the cookie.

Cool on baking sheet for 15 minutes before handling.

A Note: My son's childhood friend loved these cookies. If I made them, when he was a small boy (and teen), he would polish off a fair number!

Enjoy!

"Sleep 'til you're hungry, eat 'til you're sleepy."
--Unknown

GLUTEN FREE

Desserts

Apple Cake

Gluten & Dairy Free

4 Eggs
1 cup Canola Oil
½ cup Crushed Pineapple, canned
1 tbsp. Vanilla
1 tbsp. Apple Cider Vinegar
¼ cup Sugar
3½ cups Apples, diced and cored
2 ½ tsp. Salt
2¾ cups My Favourite 1:1 Flour*
2 tsps. Xanthan Gum
½ tsp. Baking Soda
2 tsps. Baking Powder
½ tsp. Salt
2 tsps. Cinnamon
½ tsp. Gingerbread Seasoning from Epicure, or put a dash of cloves and nutmeg if you don't have this spice blend

TOPPING
4 tbsps. Butter
½ cup Brown Sugar
¼ cup Milk (Rice Milk if Dairy Free)
1 cup Coconut, unsweetened flakes
½ cup Pecans, chopped

*Flour blend is VERY important in end product. If you decide to use a different flour blend, do NOT add the xanthan gum from this recipe if it has a gum already in it, or it will not turn out. You will find my favourite 1:1 flour in this cookbook. If you are using a premade mix, I find Kinnikinnick works the best for premade in my recipes.

In your Kitchen-Aid beat the eggs, oil, sugar, vanilla, pineapple and vinegar for two minutes.

Peel, core and dice apples. Add the apples to the egg mixture and stir.

Measure all the dry ingredients into a separate bowl and stir with a whisk. Then add the wet ingredients and mix well. Scrap sides of bowl and beat again.

Grease a large 10-inch spring from pan.

Pour the cake batter into the pan. Let it sit on the counter for 10 to 15 minutes.

Place cake into a 350°F oven and bake for 40 minutes.

I insert a knife or toothpick in the middle of the cake to make sure it is baked (it should come out clean and without dough stuck to the knife/toothpick).

Put hot cake onto cooling rack.

Then make the cake TOPPING while you wait for it to cool a bit.

> Melt the butter in a saucepan. Add the brown sugar, milk, pecans, and coconut, stir.
>
> Pour the topping over the warm cake. Place cake under the broiler for a couple of minutes until it is bubbling and golden brown.

Once the topping is done, you can spread it onto the cake, broil and eat it warm.

This cake does not need to cool completely, and it will still have great texture and taste.

Enjoy!

"We are living in a world today where lemonade is made from artificial flavors and furniture polish is made from real lemons."
--Alfred E. Newman

Donuts

Gluten Free

DONUT
- 1 cup My Favourite GF 1:1 Flour*
- ½ tsp. Xanthan Gum
- 1 tsp. Baking Soda
- 1 tsp. Baking Powder
- ¼ tsp. Cinnamon
- ¼ tsp. Salt
- 1 tbsp. Canola Oil
- 2 tsps. Vinegar
- 3 tbsps. Maple Syrup
- 1 Egg
- 5.2 oz Activia Vanilla Yogurt

ICING
- ½ cup Gluten Free Semi-Sweet Chocolate Chips
- 2 tbsps. Butter
- 1 cup Icing Sugar
- 1 to 2 tbsps. Hot Water

*Flour blend is VERY important in end product. If you decide to use a different flour blend, do NOT add the xanthan gum from this recipe if it has a gum already in it, or it will not turn out. You will find my favourite 1:1 flour in this cookbook. If you are using a premade mix, I find Kinnikinnick works the best for premade in my recipes.

Grease your donut baking pan.

In a mixing bowl measure flour, xanthan gum, baking soda, baking powder, cinnamon, and salt. Whisk well and set to the side.

In a second bowl measure and stir the vinegar, maple syrup, egg and yogurt. Pour this mixture into your dry ingredients and stir well, counting to 50 strokes.

Scoop batter into prepared donut pan. You can use a muffin/cookie scoop to evenly put into donut pan or you can put the batter into a decorating bag or ziploc bag, cut off the corner and squeeze the dough evenly into the donut pan. This is less messy and easier.

Let the filled donut pan sit for 10 minutes.

Then bake in a 400°F oven for 10 minutes. You will know they are done when they are nicely browned.

Cool for 5 minutes in the pan and then remove from pan and cool completely before you ice.

You can now ice with chocolate icing or a honey glaze. The photo shows the chocolate.

I usually make the icing while the donuts are baking. For the chocolate icing melt the chocolate and butter in a saucepan over low heat. Stir continually until melted and smooth. Then remove from the heat and stir in the icing sugar and 1 tablespoon of water. Add more hot water, just a bit at a time if the icing is too thick ... until you get the perfect consistency! If you get it too thin, then just add a bit of icing sugar to thicken it up.

Dip your cooled donuts into the chocolate icing and then set them on a cooling rack to drip and set.

These do not freeze well or store well.

Enjoy!

"Cooking is like love. It should be entered into with abandon or not at all."
--Harriet Van Horne

Strawberry Rhubarb Cobbler

Gluten Free

FILLING
2 cups Rhubarb, chopped
2 cups Strawberries, hulled and sliced
2 tbsps. Sugar
1 tsp. Cornstarch
1 tsp. Mandarin Orange Zest

COBBLER TOPPING
2 tbsps. Sugar
1 cup My Favourite GF 1:1 Flour*
1 tsp. Xanthan Gum
1 tsp. Baking Powder
1 tsp. Cinnamon
¼ tsp. Salt
¼ cup Butter, melted
½ cup Buttermilk
3 tbsps. Mandarin Orange Juice, freshly squeezed
Raw Sugar, for sprinkling on top of cobbler

*Flour blend is VERY important in end product. If you decide to use a different flour blend, do NOT add the xanthan gum from this recipe if it has a gum already in it, or it will not turn out. You will find my favourite 1:1 flour in this cookbook. If you are using a premade mix, I find Kinnikinnick works the best for premade in my recipes.

In a medium bowl, mix the rhubarb, strawberries, sugar, cornstarch, and zest. Let sit for 30 minutes to bring out the juices.

In a separate bowl, whisk together the sugar, flour, baking powder, cinnamon, xanthan gum, and salt. Add the butter, milk, egg, vanilla, and orange juice. Stir until well mixed, at least 40-50 strokes.

Scoop your strawberry mixture into individual ramekin dishes. I filled mine ¾ full and it made four desserts. Then scoop the cobbler batter on top of the fruit mixture. Sprinkle the top of each ramekin cobbler with the raw sugar.

Bake for 30-35 minutes until cobbler crust is golden brown and you can see a bit of the fruit juice bubbling up.

Serve it warm.

If you wish, serve with whipped cream, coconut cream or vanilla ice cream.

Enjoy!

"Everything I eat has been proved by some doctor or other to be a deadly poison, and everything I don't eat has been proved to be indispensable for life. But I go marching on."
--George Bernard Shaw

Pie Dough

Gluten & Dairy Free

75 grams Hard Block Margarine, I use Parkay
75 grams Butter (use all Parkay if DF is needed)
2 cups My Favourite 1:1 GF Flour*
½ tsp. Salt
½ tsp. Sugar
1 tsp. Vinegar
1 Large Egg
⅓ cup Cold Water

*Flour blend is VERY important in end product. If you decide to use a different flour blend, do NOT add the xanthan gum from this recipe if it has a gum already in it, or it will not turn out. You will find my favourite 1:1 flour in this cookbook. If you are using a premade mix, I find Kinnikinnick works the best for premade in my recipes.

Put the flour, sugar, and salt into a mixing bowl. Whisk. Weigh the butter and margarine and grate into flour mixture. Then stir with a spoon.

Add the vinegar, egg, and cold water to the mixing bowl. With a Kitchen-Aid or electric mixer, beat for approximately 2 minutes.
The mixture should not have any dry or crumbly bits.

Roll your dough out to 1/8-inch thickness and place into a pie plate or tart shell.

I use a handy rolling pin that has rings on the end that allows me to roll dough evenly, I find it works well ... but there is no problem at all to roll the dough out and estimate. I just find this rolling pin makes the job easier.

You may bake the shell and store it in the freezer for later use or fill the pie shell with a filling of your choice and bake.

In this recipe book I have included pumpkin, peach and flapper pie filling, if you are interested in trying.

If you have made a fruit pie, bake for 10 minutes at 400°F and then turn down the oven to 350°F and bake for an additional 20 minutes.

You will know the pie is done when the fruit starts to bubble.

A Note: I grew up eating pie. My dad was a professional baker and loved pie! My mom also loved pie and she was taught how to make pie by my Gramma who made the BEST pear pie.

My mom made pie for every occasion. I have many memories of us all having to hold a warm pie, that she had made, as we drove to a family gathering. She is actually the BEST pie baker that I know! The only issue is that she makes pie with gluten.

Once celiac hit, I had to figure out how to make gluten free pie. NOW, that was not easy! There were a lot of crumbled messes and crusts that were rock hard. Finally, I have the perfect crust and it always turns out.

Enjoy!

"There is nothing better on a cold wintry day than a properly made pot pie."
--Craig Claiborne

Pie-Peach

Gluten & Dairy Free

7 cups Peaches, sliced
¾ cup Sugar
3 tbsps. Minute Tapioca
1 ½ tbsps. Cornstarch
1 tsp. Cinnamon
¼ tsp. Nutmeg
1 tbsp. Milk or Rice Milk if need Dairy Free
2-3 tsps. Course Raw Sugar

Place sliced peaches in a large bowl.

Add sugar, minute tapioca, cornstarch, cinnamon, and nutmeg to peaches and stir well. Let the mixture sit on your counter as you make and roll out the pie crust.

My pie crust is in this book and is flaky and has a good texture. Make the dough and then roll it out to ¼ inch thick and place it in a pie plate and roll over and pinch the top edges along the top of the pie crust.

Pour the peach mixture into the crust and spread out evenly.

Roll out more pie dough and I like to use cookie cutters to cut out dough and place it on top of pie, I think it looks fancy and beautiful ... plus it is easier than rolling out a pie top!

Then, use a pastry brush to put a thin layer of milk on top of pie crust. Sprinkle raw sugar on top of the thin layer of milk. This is optional, but it makes the pie shimmer and brown nicely.

Bake for 15 minutes in a 425°F oven and then reduce the heat to 375°F. Bake for an additional 25 minutes. You can tell it is done when the pie filling is bubbling, and the pie crust is slightly browned.

Cool on a rack before serving. It is lovely slightly warm, or let it cool and then warm it up a bit before serving. The filling will firm up more if you let it cool. Either way, it tastes great!

A Note: With the extra pie dough, I always make some little 'hand pies' for a treat for my family. They taste great warm from the oven.

Simply roll out the extra dough and use a circle cookie cutter, or glass, and cut out circles. Then put a teaspoon or so of jam in the middle, then place a second circle on top and use a fork to seal the edges. Brush with milk and sprinkle with sugar. Bake for 25 minutes.

The tradition comes from my Gram, and my family loves it! She would always eat this little treat with us after baking pie with a cup of tea. Then have the actual pie for dinner.

Enjoy!

"Part of the secret of success in life is to eat what you like and let the food fight it out inside."
--Mark Twain

Pie- Pumpkin

Gluten Free

3 Eggs
2 cups Pumpkin Purée
½ cup Brown Sugar
½ cup Whipped Cream
1 tsp. Cinnamon
½ tsp. Ginger
¼ tsp. Cloves
Pecans(optional)
Whipped Cream for topping the pie (optional)

Place all of the ingredients, other than pecans, into a mixing bowl. I use Kitchen-Aid or electric mixer to beat the ingredients for 2 minutes. Scrape the bowl with a spatula and then beat for another minute.

Fill the pie shell with the pumpkin pie filling. Your pie shell can be bought or homemade. I think homemade is always tastier! I have included my pie crust recipe in this cookbook.

You have a few options for the top of your pie;
1. Leave the pie plain
2. Cut extra pie dough with small cookie cutters and decorate the top of the pie
3. Sprinkle top of pie with pecans
4. Candy pecans and then put on top of pie
In the photo, I have used small leaf cookie cutters, letters and candied pecans.

Bake the pie at 400°F for 15 minutes.

Then turn your oven down to 350°F and bake for 30-40 minutes.

The timing will depend on how deep you have made your pie. Take it out of the oven when you first start to see some cracks on the outer inch of pie filling.

Then let it cool completely before you serve.

We like to serve each piece with fresh whipped cream. I often sweeten my cream with a bit of maple syrup instead of sugar, it tastes nice with the pumpkin.

A Note: As for me, I could eat Pumpkin Pie anytime of the year!

Whether you make or buy your pie shells, I hope you enjoy this pumpkin pie filling!

Enjoy!

"As a child my family's menu consisted of two choices: take it or leave it."

--Buddy Hacket

Pie - Mom's Flapper Pie

Gluten Free

CRUST
2 cups Gluten Free Graham Crumbs
6 tbsps. Butter, melted

PIE FILLING
4 cups Milk
4 tbsps. Cornstarch
5 tbsps. Sugar
3 Egg Yolks
1 tsp. Vanilla
1 tbsp. Butter

TOPPING
1 cup Whipping Cream
3 tbsps. Sugar

For the crust, mix the ingredients in a bowl with a spoon. Then press evenly into a pie plate. Bake at 350°F for 15 minutes.

While your crust bakes, you can make the pudding.

In a small bowl stir cornstarch, sugar, and egg yolk. Set to the side. Add a tablespoon or two of milk from your 4 cups measure to thin egg mixture, if necessary.

Put milk into a heavy pan on stove and heat on medium heat, stir continually with a wooden spoon. If you are a celiac do not use a wooden spoon that has ever met gluten!

Once the milk is warm add a bit of the warm milk to the egg mixture and mix quickly so the yolks don't cook and become stringy.

Then add egg mixture, while stirring to the pan of milk. Bring entire mixture to a boil, over medium heat, and cook for 1 minute, stirring continually.

Stir in vanilla and butter at the very end.

Now pour the warm pudding into your prepared gluten free graham pie shell. Let the pie cool completely. Then whip cream and sugar and spread on top of pie.
Cut and serve the pie. If you are not eating the pie right away, then keep the pie in the fridge until ready to eat.

My mom made this with a meringue topping, if you would prefer then substitute for whipped cream. Use the egg whites from the pudding.

You can also serve this as pudding and not make it into a pie. It is a great pudding!

Makes me feel like a kid again.

Enjoy!

"The most remarkable thing about my mother is that for thirty years she served the family nothing but leftovers.
The original meal has never been found."
--Calvin Trillin

Apple Pear Crisp

Gluten, Dairy & Egg Free

2.5 cups Apples, cored and sliced
2.5 cups Pears, cored and sliced

TOPPING
¼ cup Brown Rice Flour
2 tbsp. Millet
2 tbsp. Sorghum
2 tbsp. Amaranth
½ cup Oats
½ cup GF Oats
½ cup Brown Sugar
½ tsp. Cinnamon
½ tsp. Nutmeg
⅓ cup Pecans, chopped
½ cup Butter

Peel, core and slice the apples and pears. Place them into a casserole baking dish or pie plate.

In a bowl measure and mix all the dry ingredients. Cut the butter on top of the dry ingredients. Use your hands to mix the butter into the dry ingredients by rubbing your hands back and forth gently. Once the mixture is well combined, it will be lumpy, then sprinkle it evenly on top of the apples/ pears.

Bake crisp in a 350°F oven for 45 minutes.

Enjoy!

A Note: Growing up, CRISP was a staple in our home. My mom made apple or berry crisp at least once a week.

If you don't have a lot of time, substitute the apples with frozen berries and it will save a lot of time and it tastes amazing! If you do not have millet, sorghum and amaranth ... then substitute the amounts with rice and oat flour.

Whenever I make crisp, I think the smells make the home feel cozy and warm.

Enjoy!

Brownies with Naturally Flavored Raspberry Icing

Gluten Free

¾ cup My Favourite Gluten Free 1:1 Flour*
1 tsp. Baking Powder
¼ tsp. Salt
½ tsp. Xanthan Gum
½ cup Butter
1 cup Chocolate Chips
½ cup Sugar
3 Eggs
1 tsp. Vanilla

RASPERRY ICING
1 cup Butter, softened
1 cup Frozen Raspberries, look at instructions on how to separate juice

*Flour blend is VERY important in end product. If you decide to use a different flour blend, do NOT add the xanthan gum from this recipe if it has a gum already in it, or it will not turn out. You will find my favourite 1:1 flour in this cookbook. If you are using a premade mix, I find Kinnikinnick works the best for premade in my recipes.

Defrost the frozen raspberries in your microwave, then place in a sieve that is placed over a bowl/measuring cup to catch the liquid. Set to the side while you make your brownies. You will use this for the icing.

Melt the chocolate and butter in the microwave. Stir and set to the side to cool.

In a bowl, measure and whisk the flour, baking powder, salt, and xanthan gum.

In a second bowl measure and beat your eggs, sugar, and vanilla. Add your egg mixture to the flour mixture and stir.

Now, add your chocolate mixture and mix well.

I have a small 9.5×13.5-inch baking/cookie sheet that I use for these chocolate heart brownies. Grease the pan and line with parchment paper, this allows you to be able to easily transfer it to a cutting board later.

I use my scoop to place 'scoops of batter' all over the parchment ... it makes one's life easier when spreading the dough! Spread the batter evenly in the pan.

Bake in a 350°F oven for 20 minutes.

Take out of oven and let cool for 15 minutes.

While the brownies cool, you can make the butter icing.

Mash the raspberries with the edge of a spoon in the sieve and push more of the liquid out of the raspberries.

Cream the butter and then add the strained raspberries. The icing will be a lovely pink and have a wonderful raspberry flavor.

I find I don't usually need to add any of the separated juice, but if your icing is too thick just add a teaspoon of the reserved juice at a time to make it the consistency that you would like. It should be thick and creamy.

Transfer the cooled brownies to a cutting board. Use a heart cookie cutter (or any shape you would like!) and cut out the brownies. Then use a serrated knife to slice the brownie hearts in half horizontally, to be able to pipe in the icing.

Fill your piping bag with icing, and I use a round tip. If you don't have a piping bag or tip, just use a sandwich bag and cut a small corner out of the edge .. it works!

Cover one side of the heart with icing and then place the other side of the heart on top. You can serve the brownie just like that, or I like to sprinkle with a dusting of icing sugar... I find it adds a nice touch!

I have an icing duster that was given to me as a gift and I

love it. I have never found one just like it ... so if you do not have such a gadget ... your fingers will work just fine for sprinkling! You can really decorate these however you would like.

A Note: I make up a 'heart brownie' for each person in my family and then I leave the raspberry icing bag in the fridge for my hubby and teens to enjoy filling their own brownie with fresh raspberry butter-cream icing. One brownie at a time ... whenever they want one!

This way each person can put as much or as little icing on as they want!

I'm sure you can guess that my diabetic hubby uses very little icing, and the teens load it up!

Enjoy!

"A recipe has no soul. You as the cook must bring soul to the recipe.
--Thomas Keller

Chocolate Cake (Easy)

Gluten Free

1 pkg. Betty Crocker, Compliments or Kinnikinnick Chocolate Cake Mix*
1 pkg. Instant Chocolate Jello Pudding Mix
¾ cup Chocolate Chips
1 cup Sour Cream
½ cup Canola Oil
1 cup Warm Water
4 Eggs

*I have used the three listed cake mixes and I know that they work. I am sure many cake mixes would work fine, I just have not tried!

Put all of your ingredients into your Kitchen-aid mixing bowl. Beat for 1 minute. Scrape the sides of bowl and then beat for another minute.

I have a muffin scoop and I use it to scoop the dough into paper lined muffin pan. This recipe makes 24 cupcakes. Let the scooped cupcakes sit in the pan for 15 minutes.

Bake cupcakes for 25 minutes in a 350°F oven.

Cool for 10 minutes in the pan on a cooling rack. Then remove cupcakes from pan and cool completely on cooling rack.

A Note: This is a recipe that was given to me years ago. It is so easy to make, and it tastes wonderful.

I sometimes cut the cupcakes in half, horizontally, then spoon some whipped cream and cherries in the middle and on top and then sprinkle with some shaved chocolate. We call it deconstructed black forest cake!

Enjoy!

Butter Cream Icing

Gluten & Egg Free

1 cup Butter, room temperature
1 tbsp. Vanilla
4 cups Icing Sugar
4 tbsps. Milk or Cream
2-3 drops Food Coloring, optional

Cream butter in your Kitchen-aid until smooth.

Scrape the sides of mixing bowl and add the vanilla, icing sugar and milk/cream. Turn your mixer on very slowly or you will be covered in icing sugar! Beat on low until combined and then turn your mixer up to medium speed until icing is smooth.

If the icing seems a bit thick, add an extra tablespoon of milk at a time and then beat until you get to the consistency you desire.

"After dinner sit a while, and after supper walk a mile."
--English Saying

Carrot Cake

Gluten Free

2 cups My Favourite 1:1 Gluten Free Flour
1 tsp. Xanthan Gum
1 tsp. Baking Soda
1 ½ tsp. Baking Powder
½ tsp. Salt
2 tsps. Cinnamon
½ cup Sugar
⅓ cup Brown Sugar
3 cups Carrots, grated
½ cup Canola Oil
4 Eggs, room temperature
1 tsp. Apple Cider Vinegar
½ cup Milk

*Flour blend is VERY important in end product. If you decide to use a different flour blend, do NOT add the xanthan gum from this recipe if it has a gum already in it, or it will not turn out. You will find my favourite 1:1 flour in this cookbook. If you are using a premade mix, I find Kinnikinnick works the best for premade in my recipes.

Measure all the dry ingredients into a bowl and mix well. Set to the side.

Put the milk and apple cider vinegar into your Kitchen-aid mixing bowl and set to the side.

Grate the carrots and place them in the milk bowl. Add oil and slightly beaten eggs to the milk bowl and mix well.

Add the dry ingredients to the Kitchen-aid bowl and mix for 2 minutes.

Cover your bowl for 10 minutes and let dough rest. Then beat for 30 seconds. Scoop dough into greased or lined muffin cups or a bundt cake pan. Let the pan that is filled with dough sit for 5 minutes. Then place into a 350° F oven.

Cupcakes bake for 20 about minutes and a bundt cake takes about 45 minutes.

Cool completely before eating.

I make a simple icing sugar and water glaze and pour it over the bundt cake, while warm. Or I make cream cheese icing for the cupcakes. The recipe for the cream cheese icing is in this book.

A Note: My husband loves this as a bundt cake without cream cheese icing. I also have a pan that makes individual bundt cakes.

If I make the cupcakes, then I make cream cheese icing to go with them. I leave a few cupcakes free from icing for my hubby.

Enjoy!

"If you are a chef, no matter how good a chef you are, it's not good cooking for yourself; the joy is cooking for others. It's the same with music"

--will. i. am

Cream Cheese Icing

Gluten & Egg Free

8 oz Cream Cheese, room temperature
2 tbsps. Butter, room temperature
2½ cups Icing Sugar

In your Kitchen-aid mixing bowl, beat the cream cheese and butter and until smooth.

Slowly add the icing sugar with the mixer on low. Mix until smooth and well combined.

This icing is great on carrot cake or cinnamon buns.

Enjoy!

Chocolate Pudding

Gluten Free

3 cups Milk
3 tbsps. Cocoa
2 tbsps. Cornstarch
½ cup Sugar
1 Egg

In a small bowl stir cornstarch, sugar, cocoa, and egg. Set to the side.

Put milk in a heavy pan on stove and heat on medium heat, stir continually.

Once milk starts to get warm ... add a bit of the warm milk into the egg mixture and stir quickly so the yolk does not cook and become stringy. Then add this mixture, while stirring into the warm milk in the pan.

Keep stirring milk mixture until it comes to a boil, then cook for 1 minute and then remove from heat.

Do not stop stirring while cooking pudding, as it will burn!

Pudding can be eaten warm or cold.

A Note: My mom made chocolate pudding often when I grew up. I loved eating it warm. Definity makes me feel like I am a kid again when I eat!

Enjoy!

Date Squares

Gluten, Dairy & Egg Free

CRUST
½ cup Brown Rice Flour
2 tbsp. Millet Flour
2 tbsps. Sorghum Flour
2 tbsps. Amaranth Flour
2 tbsp. White Rice Flour
1 cup Gluten Free Oats
¼ cup Brown Sugar
½ cup Butter
1 tsp. Vanilla

FILLING
650 grams Dates, chopped
1 cup Water
¼ cup Orange Juice

Make sure your dates are pitted. Then put chopped dates and water into saucepan. Cook on medium heat for 6 to 8 minutes, stirring constantly. Remove from heat and stir in the orange juice. Set to the side.

In a mixing bowl, add the brown rice flour, millet flour, sorghum flour, amaranth flour, white rice flour, gluten free oats and brown sugar. Stir to ensure it is well combined. Then add cut up butter and vanilla to dry ingredients. Rub mixture back and forth in your hands until crumbly and evenly combined.   Place 2/3 of the crumbled mixture into the bottom of a greased 8x8 pan. Press this mixture down, evenly, with the palm of your hand.

Then spread the date filling evenly on top of crumble mixture. Sprinkle the remaining crumb mixture over the dates and then lightly press with the palm of your hand.

Bake date squares in a 350° F oven for 20-25 minutes.

You will be able to tell it's done when the edges are getting a bit brown. Let it cool completely, or they will be very soft and hard to handle. Cut into squares. I keep them in the freezer, with wax paper between the layers. Cut them ahead and separate them, this makes it easy to grab a few for a Christmas baking tray.

A Note: My Gramma had date squares in a tin on her counter often when I would go to visit.

Date squares are a treat that I have always loved. Since revamping the original recipe, I now add many different gluten free grains to the squares to increase nutrients, fibre and flavour.

My non-celiac sister absolutely loves this recipe, she even makes it with all the unique gluten free grains instead of 'normal' flour ... she says it's better!

Enjoy,
Teresa

"Cooking is at once child's play and adult joy
And cooking done with care is an act of love. ."
--Craig Claiborne

Great Gram's Raspberry Dessert

Gluten & Egg Free

1 package Raspberry JELLO, you can use sugar free if needed
1 cup Boiling Water
2 cups Ice Cubes
1.5 cups Kinnikinnick Graham Style crumbs
1 cup Whipping Cream, not whipped
2 tbsps. Sugar
½ cup Fresh or Frozen Raspberries

Put JELLO powder into a bowl and add boiling water. Stir well until powder has dissolved. Add ice cubes and stir for 2 minutes and then take out the remaining ice cubes. Put JELLO into fridge.

Evenly spread Graham Crumbs into a 9×13 pan and press flat with the palm of your hand. Set to the side. Or put a couple tablespoons in the bottom of a pretty glass cup, glass bowl or jar, to make individual servings.

Sometimes I drive all around town and cannot find the graham style crumbs and then I do one of two things...

Forget the crumbs and just make it without!
OR
Bake my chocolate chip cookies (in this book) and then crumble them up in place of graham style crumbs.

Whip the cream and sugar, set to the side.

Once the JELLO is just starting to thicken, then gently stir in ¾ of prepared whipped cream. The remainder of cream can be put back into fridge for later.

Pour JELLO mixture on top of prepared graham crust and sprinkle with a few extra crumbs from your box of crumbs. Cover and place into the fridge to get firm.

Once it is firm, serve with a spoon of leftover cream on top with a few raspberries for decoration.

A Note: My Gram and mom made this 100's of times in my life. It really is very simple and tastes great.

We have made this dessert a tradition when we go camping. I put it into individual size tupperware containers with a lid. Then, each person can eat as much as they want out of their own container. The kids loved this when they were growing up!

They are pretty much grown up now ... and they still love it!

ENJOY!

"Life is uncertain. Eat dessert first."
--Ernestine Ulmer

CheeseCake

Gluten & Dairy Free

CRUST
1 cup Gluten Free Chocolate Cookie Crumbs
¼ cup Hard Block Margarine, melted

FILLING
4 blocks (225 grams each) Dairy Free Cream Cheese, try the brand Plant Head
2 Eggs
¾ cup Sugar
1 tbsp. Lemon Rind, grated
2 tbsps. Lemon Juice
½ teaspoon Almond Extract
2 tbsps. Cornstarch or Arrowroot Powder

TOPPING
Berries
Chocolate Sauce

Mix the crust ingredients and then press into a pie plate or 8-inch spring form pan.

In a Kitchen-aid mixing bowl mix the cream cheese until smooth. Then add the other filling ingredients and mix well.

Scrape filling into prepared crumb crust and spread gently so that it is even across pie plate.

Bake in a preheated oven of 350°F for 1 hour. Do not open the oven. Turn off the oven and leave the cheesecake in the oven for an additional hour.

Take out of oven and let cool completely on cooling rack before serving.

You can serve the cheesecake with berries, chocolate sauce or both!

Enjoy!

Plum Crumble

Gluten, Dairy & Egg Free

1 pound Plums, pitted and quartered
¼ cup Brown Rice Flour
¼ cup Gluten Free Oat Flour
¼ cup White Sugar
¼ cup Brown Sugar
⅓ cup Gluten Free Oats
¼ cup Almonds, sliced
⅓ cup Hard Block Margarine, I use Parkay (cut into cubes)

In a 9" round greased pie plate, place the plums.

In a bowl measure and mix the brown rice flour, gluten free oat flour, sugars, gluten free oats and almonds. Cut the margarine into the dry ingredients and then rub the mixture with your hands until crumbly and well combined. Sprinkle the crumb mixture on top of the plums.

Bake in a 375°F oven for 45 minutes, it should be bubbling up through the top when it is done.

Take it out of oven and let it cool on a cooling rack.

A Note: We have a prune plum tree on our acreage. In the fall, when the plums become ripe, we have hundreds that we need to eat!

The plums get eaten in lunches and snacks ... and I always make at least one of these plum crumbles. We all love it but my husband absolutely loves this crumble with our fresh picked plums from our tree!

Eat it warm with ice cream...... soooooo good!

Enjoy!

Individual Blueberry Crisp

Gluten, Dairy & Egg Free

3/4 cup Blueberries (frozen or fresh)
1 tbsp. Buckwheat Flour
1 tbsp. Millet Flour
1/4 cup Quinoa Flakes
1 tbsp. Brown Sugar
1 tsp. Cinnamon
1 tbsp. Butter, cut up (use DF Butter if needed)

Put the blueberries into a ramekin dish. I used frozen blueberries.

In a separate bowl measure, the buckwheat flour, millet flour, quinoa flakes, cinnamon and brown sugar.

Cut the butter into the dry ingredients and use your hands to rub and evenly incorporate it in. Then spread the crumble mixture on top of the blueberries. You could sprinkle some cinnamon and brown sugar on top for decoration if you wish.

Bake for 30 minutes in 375°F oven.

Serve it warm.

A Note: I made this recipe for a family member who is on a keto diet. I just substituted the brown sugar for monk sugar, and he said it was delicious.

Enjoy!

Ice Cream Sandwiches

Gluten Free

COOKIE
1 cup HardBlock Margarine, I use Parkay
1⅓ cup Sugar
1 tsp. Salt
4 Egg Yolks
116 grams Cocoa
½ tsp. Baking Powder
2 tsp. Xanthan Gum
4 tsps. Vanilla
340 grams My Favourite GF 1:1 Flour*
1 tsp. Xanthan Gum
1½ cup Hot Water

ICECREAM
Pick whatever flavours you wish, you can choose gluten free, dairy free, nut free ... whatever your family needs and likes!

*Flour blend is VERY important in end product. If you decide to use a different flour blend, do NOT add the xanthan gum from this recipe if it has a gum already in it, or it will not turn out. You will find my favourite 1:1 flour in this cookbook. If you are using a premade mix, I find Kinnikinnick works the best for premade in my recipes.

I weigh my flour and cocoa powder in this recipe, as it turns out the best and needs to be accurate.

In a bowl mix the flour, xanthan gum and cocoa. Set to the side.

Add the butter, sugar, salt, baking powder and vanilla to your Kitchen-aid mixing bowl and beat until creamed.

Slowly add egg yolk to the butter mixture, one at a time.

Slowly add the dry mixture to the butter mixture. Mix well. The dough will be very thick.

CAREFULLY add the hot water to the batter, stir very slowly or it will splash all over you. Be careful not to burn yourself. Once it is incorporated, then beat for 5 minutes (set timer!). Batter will be very smooth!

To make the cookie portion of the ice cream sandwich you have a couple of options.

OPTION#1
Spread the dough on a parchment lined cookie sheet and bake at 375°F for 15 minutes. Then use a circle cookie cutter and cut out as many circles as you can.

OPTION#2
Draw circles on a parchment (you could trace the cookie cutter). Then put a scoop of dough onto each circle and spread dough out to fill in the circle, getting it as even as possible. Bake at 375°F for 8 to 10 minutes.

If you choose option #1 you will have more wasted batter but it is a much faster choice.

For the ice cream part of the sandwich, I put parchment or plastic wrap in a cake pan and then scoop and flatten my ice cream of choice into the pan trying to make it 1 to 1½ inch thick. I then put this pan back into the freezer until it is firm. Take out the pan and use plastic wrap or parchment paper to lift the ice cream out. Cut out circles of ice cream ... I have a deep round cookie cutter that is 2 inches deep, so I can use it to cut the circles. If you do not have a cookie cutter, you could cut the cookies and ice cream into squares or rectangles instead! If your house is warm, make sure to put your ice cream discs back into the freezer if they are starting to melt.

Once you have cut out all of your ice cream discs and cookies, put a cookie on each side of the disc and put it on a parchment lined baking sheet and freeze your sandwiches. Leave them in the freezer

individually in the wax paper and use the plastic wrap to make it tight.

For at least an hour to ensure firm.

I lay a piece of saran wrap on my counter and then wax paper on top of that. Then I wrap each ice cream sandwich.

I then place the sandwiches into a ziploc or container with a lid and put them back into the freezer. If they are melting, then work faster! :)

I separate or label the dairy free sandwiches. Freeze until ready to eat. They are now ready to be enjoyed over the summer.

A Note: You can make these ahead and take one out at a time and enjoy. You can even take them camping if you have a freezer. If your campground or local ice cream shop is not safe for your celiac or dairy free person ... they have a nice treat to enjoy by the lake!

For the ice cream part of the sandwich, you can use dairy free or regular ice cream.

I always make a few dairy free ice cream sandwiches for my hubby and the rest regular ice cream.

It's nice to have options to make each person with food intolerances be able to enjoy this wonderful summertime ice cream treat!

Enjoy!

"For we brought nothing into the world and we can take nothing out of it. But if we have food and clothing, we will be content with that."

--1 Timothy 6:7-8

Pineapple Squares

Gluten & Dairy Free

BASE
1 ¼ cups My Favourite 1:1 GF All Purpose Flour*
130 grams Butter (use dairy free, if needed)
¼ cup Sugar
1 tsp. Xanthan Gum*

TOPPING
14 grams Butter (use dairy free, if needed)
½ cup Sugar
1 Egg
14 oz can Crushed Pineapple
½ cup Flaked Coconut (separated in half)

*Flour blend is VERY important in end product. If you decide to use a different flour blend, do NOT add the xanthan gum from this recipe if it has a gum already in it, or it will not turn out. My favourite 1:1 flour is in this cookbook.

Before you start, open your can of pineapple, and empty it into a sieve, and let it drain as you prepare the squares. Once in a while take a spoon, or your hand, and push on the pineapple to try to get rid of excess liquid.

BASE
Grate the butter. In a medium bowl, whisk the flour, sugar, and xanthan gum together. Then add the grated butter. Stir with a spoon. Pat down into an 8x8 inch ungreased pan. Bake for 15 minutes in a 350°F oven.

TOPPING
While the base is in the oven, prepare the topping. Cream together the butter, sugar, and egg. Use a spoon to fold in the well-drained pineapple and 1/4 cup coconut. Mix well.

Spread this pineapple mixture evenly over the baked base, sprinkle 1/4 cup coconut over the top. Return the pineapple squares to the oven and bake for 20-25 minutes. Let them cool completely before cutting.

I keep these squares in the freezer, as they defrost quickly. I cut it into squares and then put wax paper between the layers. They are great to add to a Christmas baking tray.

A Note: My mom made pineapple squares when I was growing up. Once I was diagnosed celiac, she never made them again. My children had never had pineapple squares.

In 2020, my sister made some gluten free pineapple squares. The kids loved them so much that they were hiding in her boot-room with her …. hoping I would not see them eating the squares before dinner! As they all came into the kitchen, they were wiping the crumbs off their face trying to look innocent.

So, I HAD to get her recipe and include it in our family book. Hopefully you enjoy these squares, as much as my kids! I did change a thing or two … so her's will always be THEE BEST to my kids!

Enjoy,
Teresa

"A generous person will prosper, whoever refreshes others will be refreshed."
--Proverbs 11:25

Cherry Cake

Gluten & Dairy Free

1 cup Hard Block Margarine, I use Parkay
1 cup Sugar
4 Eggs
1 tsp. Almond Extract
2 cups My Favourite 1:1 GF Flour
1 tsp. Xanthan Gum
1 tbsp. Baking Powder
1 can Cherry Pie Filling
Icing Sugar, to sprinkle over cake
Whipped Cream, for topping*

*Flour blend is VERY important in end product. If you decide to use a different flour blend, do NOT add the xanthan gum from this recipe if it has a gum already in it, or it will not turn out. You will find my favourite 1:1 flour in this cookbook. If you are using a premade mix, I find Kinnikinnick works the best for premade in my recipes.

Cream butter and sugar in Kitchen-aid. Add the eggs and beat until light and fluffy. Add the almond extract.

Stir in the flour, xanthan gum, and baking powder. Mix until smooth and then let sit for 5 minutes. Mix again for a few seconds.

Then pour batter into a greased 9x13 inch cake pan. Smooth batter evenly in pan. Use a spoon to make about 15 holes. Drop spoonful of cherry pie filling into the holes.

Bake at 350°F for 45-55 minutes. You will know it is done when you insert a knife into the middle of the cake, and it comes out clean. As soon as it comes out of the oven, dust it with icing sugar. Then let the cake cool a bit on a cooling rack.

Serve it warm with whipped cream. If you cannot have dairy, you can omit or make coconut whipped cream.

Enjoy!

Pavlova

Gluten Free with Dairy Free option

3 Egg Whites
¾ cup Sugar
1 ½ tsps. Cornstarch
1 cup Whipping Cream (not whipped)
Fruit of Choice, sliced small
Chocolate Bar, shaved or curled
4 tbsps. Sugar

Preheat oven to 325°F.

In a Kitchen-aid bowl, free from oil, crack COLD egg whites into mixing bowl. Beat until satiny peaks form. Then add ¾ cup sugar, slowly, about 1 tablespoon at a time. Beat until the meringue becomes shiny and stiff. Then take bowl of mixer and with a spatula gently fold in cornstarch.

Scoop meringue onto parchment lined baking sheets and smooth out with a knife.

Put baking sheets into preheated oven and immediately turn down heat to 275°F.

Bake for 30 minutes. Watch carefully and do not overcook. You want the inside to be like marshmallow and the outside to be crunchy. When the meringue JUST starts to crack on the very edge of the meringue ... take it out of the oven and allow it to cool for at least an hour. If your house is drafty or cold, just prop open the oven door and let the meringues cool in the oven (so they don't fall and break as they cool).

Whip the cream and add the 4 tbsps. of sugar. Decorate cooled meringues with cream, fruit, and curled chocolate.

Enjoy!

EASY Pineapple Upside Down Cake

Gluten Free

1 White Cake Mix, Compliments Brand turns out the best in this recipe

¼ cup Butter
¼ cup Brown Sugar
1 can Canned Pineapple Rings, drained

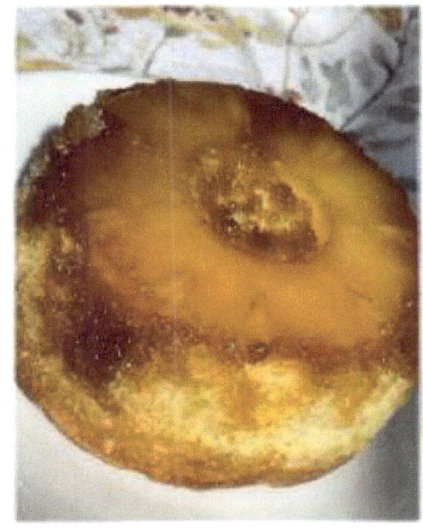

I have tried other cake mixes and have found this brand is the best for this recipe ... trust me on this one! They don't even know I am telling you about them... it is just the truth.

Make the cake batter as per the directions on the box and then set to the side as you gather the rest of the items for the cake. The cake will turn out better if you let the cake batter sit for 10-15 minutes so you do not need to rush!

You can make this cake in an 8-inch square glass cake pan or individual ramekins. I am going to give you instructions for the cake, as that is what most people will have memories of growing up with and have a cake pan. If you want to make the individual ramekins, then divide the butter, sugar, pineapple, and batter between your ramekins evenly.

Put the butter into the 8-inch glass cake pan and place in a 350°F oven. Remove the pan from the oven when the butter has completely melted. Sprinkle the sugar evenly over the melted butter. Then place the pineapple rings neatly and evenly on top of the brown sugar and butter mixture. Now, take the batter that you have already made and give it a quick stir before you evenly scoop it over the pineapple.

Place the cake in the preheated oven and bake according to the back of cake box.

Let it cool on a rack for 10 minutes and then tip it upside down onto a serving plate.

Eat it warm. It is nice with a bit of whipped cream or ice cream on the side.

Enjoy!

"It's all about a balancing act between time, temperature and ingredients. That's the art of baking."
--Peter Reinhart

Strawberry Shortcake

Gluten Free

1 cup My Favourite 1:1 GF Flour*
½ tsp. Xanthan Gum
3 tbsps. Cornstarch
1 tsp. Baking Powder
pinch Salt
⅓ cup Butter, room temperature
¾ cup Sugar
½ tsp. Almond Extract
3 Eggs, room temperature
⅔ cup Buttermilk, room temperature

*Flour blend is VERY important in end product. If you decide to use a different flour blend, do NOT add the xanthan gum from this recipe if it has a gum already in it, or it will not turn out. You will find my favourite 1:1 flour in this cookbook. If you are using a premade mix, I find Kinnikinnick works the best for premade in my recipes.

In a bowl, measure the flour, xanthan gum, cornstarch, baking powder, and salt. Then whisk and set to the side.

In your Kitchen-aid, cream the butter and sugar. Then add one egg at a time, the almond extract and buttermilk. Scrape sides. Then add the dry ingredients and mix until well combined.

I make these into individual shortcakes, they are easy to serve and look pretty. I have circle, square and heart shaped cupcake pans. You can use whatever you have. In the photo, you will see that I have used my square pan.

Bake in a 350°F oven for 20 minutes.

Cool completely before serving with whipped cream and strawberries.

If you are dairy free, use coconut whipped cream.

Enjoy

GLUTEN FREE

Miscellaneous

Macaroni and Cheese

Gluten Free

Box of Gluten Free Pasta, I used 340 g. GF Catelli

CHEESE SAUCE
¼ cup Butter
¼ cup Rice Flour
3 to 3½ cup Milk
½ tsp. Salt
¼ tsp. Pepper
¼ tsp. Oregano
½ tsp. Basil
¼ tsp. Garlic Powder
¾ cup Grated Cheese

Cook your box of pasta, as per instructions on the back of box. Drain and rinse with cold water. Put into a casserole dish.

Heat butter over medium heat in a saucepan. Once melted, add rice flour. Stir continually for 1 minute.

Slowly add milk, while stirring with a whisk. Whisk until lumps are gone and then continue stirring mixture with a spoon. Add salt, pepper, basil and oregano.

Don't stop stirring or it will burn!

Add grated cheese, save a bit to sprinkle on top of casserole.

Stir cheese sauce until bubbly and starts to thicken. If it seems a bit too thick add ¼ to ½ cup more milk.

Pour sauce over noodles, stir, and then sprinkle the top with a bit of cheese.

Bake in a 350°F degree oven for 20 minutes.

Enjoy!

Stuffing

Gluten, Dairy & Egg Free

1 ½ to 2 Loaves of Gluten Free Bread - I use Mom's Loaf*
2 tbsps. Butter or Oil
1 Onion, chopped fine
¼ cup Craisins
¼ cup Raisins
½ cup Dried Apricots, diced
2 Figs, diced
1 Apple, cored & diced
¾ cup Celery, diced
3 cloves Garlic, minced
1 tsp. Rosemary
1 tsp. Thyme
1 tsp. Sage
½ tsp. Salt
½ tsp. Pepper
¾ to 1 cup GF Chicken Stock OR GF Mushroom Soup. I use homemade or Epicures stock. I prefer the taste and texture of stock plus it's dairy free, but others like the mushroom soup. You can decide for your family.

Stuffing can be prepped up to 24 hours ahead of time. Hold back the chicken stock or mushroom soup just prior to stuffing the bird or baking it in a casserole dish.

In a skillet, heat butter over medium heat. Sauté onions, celery, and garlic until golden. Approximately 5 minutes. In a large bowl toss together cubed bread, cooled onion mixture, cranberries, raisins, apricots, apple, herbs, salt & pepper.

Add chicken stock (or mushroom soup) just prior to stuffing the bird or baking it in a casserole dish.

Clean, rinse and pat dry the turkey or chicken. Stuff bird with stuffing. Any extra stuffing you have, put it in to a greased casserole dish with a lid or foil. Place the stuffed turkey into the roasting pan and follow cooking instructions for a turkey, based on the weight of your turkey. You want to make sure the inside of the bird/stuffing comes to the correct temperature, to avoid food poisoning. Use a thermometer to ensure it has reached the proper temperature.

If cooking in a casserole dish, you will need to bake about 45-60 minutes at 400°F. Last 5-10 minutes leave lid off to brown.

A Note: *I use a loaf called 'Mom's Loaf'. The loaf is dairy, gluten and egg free and it tastes great in this recipe. If you do not have time to bake, you can use bread of your choice. I have found Northern Bakehouse has turned out well when I don't have time to bake either! I can find it in my local grocery stores or Costco.

We make this recipe for the entire extended family, and everyone likes it!

Enjoy,
Teresa

"If you really want to make a friend, go to someone's house and eat ... the people who give you their food give you their heart."

--Cesar Chavez

Brown Flour

Gluten, Dairy & Egg Free

1 cup Brown Flour
1 cup Sorghum Flour
¾ cup Tapioca Starch
½ cup Potato Starch

Use a kitchen scale to measure your ingredients. Stir well using a spoon and a whisk. Then place in an airtight container to keep your flour fresh. I store mine in the freezer so that the flour lasts longer and stays fresh.

Remember to whisk your flour each time you use it to ensure it is well mixed. Due to the different flours and starches, they can separate out while in the container.

This flour does not have xanthan gum in it, which I like because you do not always need xanthan gum in every recipe. Remember you may need to add xanthan gum to recipes to make them turn out, I usually add 1/2 to 1 teaspoon per cup, if needed.

A Note: Measuring out flour to make GF Flour mixes is not my favourite. It is not hard, I just don't like measuring it all to be able to make a recipe.

Therefore, I make up two to three batches of flour mixes at a time and store it in a sealed container. I find it makes baking less daunting, knowing that you have flour already made up.

It is important to check your flours are certified gluten free and made from a mill that does not also use gluten! Or you will be cross contaminated.

Enjoy!

"When I go to a restaurant, I always ask for a chicken and an egg, to see which comes first."
--Unknown

My Favourite 1:1 Gluten Free Flour

Gluten, Dairy & Egg Free

294 grams White Rice Flour
92 grams Brown Rice Flour
86 grams Potato Starch
37 grams Tapioca Starch

Ensure all your flours and starches are gluten free and ground on a gluten free mill.

Use a kitchen scale to measure your ingredients, so that the flour mixture is exact.

Stir well using a spoon and a whisk. Then place in an airtight container to keep your flour fresh. I store mine in the freezer to prolong freshness.

Remember to whisk your flour each time you use it to ensure it is well mixed. Due to the different flours and starches, they can separate out while in the container.

This flour does not have xanthan gum in it, which I like because you do not always need xanthan gum in every recipe. Remember you may need to add xanthan gum to recipes to make them turn out, I usually add 1/2 to 1 teaspoon per cup.

*Flour blends are VERY important and the end product will vary greatly if you use different blends in your recipes. If you decide to use a premade flour blend for recipes in this book, I suggest using Kinnikinnick's 1:1 blend, as from my experience, it turns out the best for premade. Just my honest opinion.

A Note: Gluten Free flour makes or breaks your recipe. I have tested al of my recipes with other 1:1 store bought flour blends and each one will make the recipe turn out different.

This blend truly makes baked goods taste great and have wonderful texture. I don't love weighing and making flour, but if you make a container ahead ... you will appreciate that it is ready when you want to bake. I often multiply this recipe by 2 or 3 and make a big batch at one time.

Then you are ready to bake when you feel like it!

Enjoy!

"Red meat is not bad for you. Now blue-green meat, that's bad for you!"
--Tommy Smothers

Fish Sticks

Gluten & Dairy Free

6 Tilapia Fillets
1 ½ cups Sweet Potato Crackers from Costco, ground
¼ tsp. Pepper
1 tsp. Garlic Powder
1 tsp. Thyme, dried
1 tsp. Basil, dried
1 tsp. Paprika
2 Eggs, beaten with a fork
1 cup Rice Flour

I buy frozen tilapia fillets, it is easier to cut them when they are half frozen. Cut the fillets into 4 long pieces to make the 'sticks.'

Place the rice flour in a pie plate.

Place the beaten eggs in a pie plate.

Grind sweet potato crackers and place in a pie plate. I just use a blender, handheld food processor or magic bullet to grind the crackers.

Add all other dry ingredients to the ground crackers and stir well.

Dip your fish pieces into the rice flour. I do all the pieces at one time, as it is less messy.

Then dip all your floured pieces into the egg mixture.

Take your egg dipped fish pieces and 'roll' in the cracker mixture. Make sure to get all sides of the fish covered. Place them on a parchment lined baking sheet.

Bake at 400°F for 15 minutes or until golden.

Serve hot.

We eat these with homemade Oven Baked Fries. You will find the Oven Baked Fries recipe in this book.

Enjoy!

"A crust eaten in peace is better than a banquet partaken in anxiety."
--Aesop

Oven Baked Fries

Gluten, Dairy & Egg Free

4 small Sweet Potatoes, sliced in rounds ⅛ " thick
2 small Potatoes, sliced in rounds ⅛" thick
1 tbsp. Olive Oil
Salt
Pepper

Sweet potatoes are so healthy and great for your gut! Plus, they look pretty with the regular potatoes.

Cut the sweet potatoes and potatoes into approximately ⅛ thick circles/slices. You can use a knife, but I use a wavy vegetable cutter, it makes them look fancy!

Then I place the two kinds of potatoes in a bag or bowl to toss with oil, as it is less messy.

Spread the sweet potatoes and potatoes on a baking sheet. If you do NOT line it with parchment, then it will brown and leave lines from your wavy cutter.

Sprinkle with salt and pepper.

Bake at 400°F for 45 minutes to an hour. I flip potatoes every 15 to 20 minutes.

You can use these as a side to many different meals. One that it goes nicely with is the Oven Baked Fish Sticks.

Enjoy!

Games Night Dip

Gluten Free

1 package of Cream Cheese (8 oz)
½ cup Mayonnaise
7 drops Franks Hot Sauce (or hot sauce of your choice)
¼ tsp. Garlic Salt
1 can Artichokes, drained and chopped
2 cups Cheddar Cheese, grated
¼ to ⅓ cup Cherry Tomatoes, quartered
3 Green Onions, finely chopped

With your electric mixer, beat mayonnaise, cream cheese, hot sauce, and garlic salt. Beat until smooth. Then mix in 1 3/4 cup cheese and artichokes.

Spread creamy mixture into a pie plate.

Sprinkle with green onions, tomatoes, and the remaining 1/4 cup cheese.

Bake 15 to 20 minutes at 375°F.

You will know the dip is done when it has started to bubble and has browned slightly on the edges.

Serve warm with Tostitos or gluten free crackers.

A Note: My sister has made this dip for years. My son loves it so very much! It goes well with a game's night with cousins and extended family!

You can make it earlier in the day and then just throw it in the oven when you are ready to play games!

Enjoy,
Teresa

Granola Bars

Gluten, Dairy & Egg Free

140 grams Peanut Butter
110 grams Honey
1 Egg
1 tsp. Vanilla

DRY Ingredients
3 cups Gluten Free Rolled Oats
½ cup Quinoa Flakes
2 tbsps. Chia, whole
1 tbsp. Flax Seeds, whole
¼ cup Brown Sugar
⅓ cup Craisins
2 tbsps. Dried Apricots, chopped
⅓ cup Chocolate Chips

I like to measure my peanut butter and honey with a digital scale, as it makes it quicker and less messy.

Measure your peanut butter, vanilla, honey, and egg into a bowl and mix well with a spoon. Set to the side.

Measure all your DRY ingredients into a separate large bowl. Stir well with a spoon.

Add wet ingredients to your dry ingredients and stir well.

Take a small scoop and fill Snack Pan cavities, from pampered chef, with granola mixture. I put three small scoops into each cavity. I got my pan from a friend, and it is fabulous!

I wet the tips of my fingers with water and push the granola flat into the granola bar cavities, so they are flat.

With the extra granola, you can scoop it into small silicone muffin pans. A small scoop measures perfectly. Then you will have bite size granola bites!

Bake in a 350°F oven for 10-12 minutes. The edges will be just slightly golden. They will be a bit chewy. If you bake longer, they will be a crispy granola bar.

Cool on a rack.

Once completely cooled, store in an airtight container.

Enjoy!

"After all the trouble you go to, you get about as much actual "food" out of eating an artichoke as you would from licking 30 or 40 postage stamps."
--Miss Piggy

Croutons

Gluten, Dairy & Egg Free

2 cups Gluten Free Bread, I use store Northern Bakehouse or homemade
¼ cup Olive Oil
¼ tsp. Salt
½ tsp. Garlic Powder
½ tsp. Onion Powder
1/4 tsp. Basil

Use a serrated knife and cut the crusts off the bread. Then cut the bread into cubes.

I cut the bread when it is still a bit frozen, as I find it to be an easier job!

Put cut up bread into a large bowl. Mix the other ingredients in a measuring cup. Pour over bread cubes and mix well.

You can cook the croutons two different ways, depending on if you are in a rush!

OPTION #1
Spread bread mixture over parchment lined baking sheet. Bake for 45 mins in a 250°F oven. Stir halfway through the baking.

OPTION #2

Put the bread mixture into a frying pan on the stove. Stir occasionally on low-medium heat until croutons are dried and golden.

The smell is amazing ... and hard to resist the warm croutons!

A Note: Caesar salad is not complete without croutons!

These can be used immediately or stored in an airtight container in the freezer.

Enjoy!

"Do not work for food that spoils, but for food that endures to eternal life."
--John 6:27

Granola On The Go

Gluten, Dairy & Egg Free

DRY INGREDIENTS
100 grams Quinoa
200 grams Gluten Free Oats
50 grams Quinoa Flakes
25 grams Chia
100 grams Pecans, chopped
35 grams Coconut, unsweetened
50 grams Almonds, sliced

WET INGREDIENTS
½ cup Maple Syrup
2 tbsps. Honey
2 tsps. Cinnamon
1 tsp. Vanilla

DRIED FRUIT
40 grams Raisins
40 grams Craisins
40 grams Dried Apricots, cut into small chunks
25 grams Dates, chopped

Measure the DRY ingredients into a large bowl, mix and set to the side.

In a measuring cup measure the WET ingredients and stir.

Add the wet ingredients to the dry ingredients and mix well.

Spread the granola onto a parchment lined baking sheet and bake for 10 minutes in a 350°F oven. Then stir. Bake for an additional 5 minutes. Stir again and bake for another 2-3 minutes.

Take out of oven and place on a cooling rack. Immediately stir in the DRIED FRUIT.

Stir a couple of times while it cools. Once cooled, store in an airtight container. It is very good on a yogurt parfait, cereal.

or just eaten by the handful!

A Note: We call it 'Granola On the Go' because it is easy to throw on top of breakfast, lunch or a shack when you are on the run or on the go.

Take a small container or bag of this granola with you when you go out for your day ... add it to a lunch or breakfast when you are out and about.

This granola adds a lot of nutrients, fibre and energy to your snack or meal.

Enjoy!

> *"He that gives food to every creature, His love endures forever."*
> *--Psalms 136:25*

Pizza Crust

Gluten, Dairy & Egg Free

- 2 cups Warm Water, 110°F
- 1 tbsp. Instant Yeast
- ½ tbsp. Maple Syrup
- ½ tbsp. Honey
- 2 tbsp. Olive Oil
- 2 cups Brown Rice Flour
- ¾ cup Tapioca Starch
- 1 tsp. Italian Seasoning
- ½ tsp. Garlic Powder
- 1 tsp. Salt
- ¼ cup White Chia, ground not whole
- ¼ cup Flax Meal
- ¼ cup Whole Psyllium Husk, not powdered
- 1 tbsp. Olive Oil, for brushing

In a measuring cup take the temperature of the water and make sure it is 110°F. Then, add maple syrup, honey, oil & yeast, stir gently. Set to the side while you gather other ingredients.

In a Kitchen-aid mixing bowl add your rice flour, tapioca starch, spices, and salt. Mix.

Add the chia, flax and psyllium husk to the water mixture and stir. Let sit for 60 seconds (no more or it will go solid!) and then stir again. Quickly, pour the chia water mixture into the flour mixture and beat with a Kitchen-aid paddle for 3 MINUTES. Set your timer!

Preheat oven to 400°F.

Cut the dough into 7 or 8 equal lumps. I use a scale to make them exact. Put the dough onto a lightly floured pastry mat and shape each lump into an individual pizza. I use the palm of my hand and fingers to push the dough into shape, the dough is very easy to work with. We shape the dough into hearts on Valentines Day, but normally just do a circle.

Place the pizza crusts on to parchment lined cookie sheets.

Brush with a bit of oil and let sit for 10 minutes. Then bake in a 400°F oven for 10 minutes. Let your family members put sauce and toppings on of their choice. Then cook for an additional 10-15 minutes.

Cut immediately and enjoy with a side salad.

Enjoy!

"Food is an important part of a balanced diet."
--Fran Lebowitz

Sausage Rolls

Gluten Free

375 gram Gluten Free Pork Sausage, the small sausages not the big ones

1 cup plus 1 tbsp. My Favourite GF 1:1 Flour*
1 tsp. Xanthan Gum
37.5 grams Butter, grated
37.5 grams Hard Block Margarine, I use Parkay (grated)
¼ tsp. Salt
¼ tsp. Sugar
½ tsp. Vinegar
1 Egg
2 tbsps. Cold Water

1 tbsp. Milk, for brushing tops of sausages

Poke each sausage with a knife and take the skin off. This can take a bit of time but make sure to de-skin each sausage. Set the sausage in the fridge while you make the pastry.

For the pastry, a reminder that *Flour blend is VERY important in end product. If you decide to use a different flour blend, do NOT add the xanthan gum from this recipe if it has a gum already in it, or it will not turn out. You will find my favourite 1:1 flour in this cookbook. If you are using a premade mix, I find Kinnikinnick works the best for premade in my recipes.

Put the flour, sugar, xanthan gum and salt into a mixing bowl. Whisk. Weigh the butter and margarine and grate into flour mixture. Then stir with a spoon.

Add the vinegar, egg and cold water to the mixing bowl. With a Kitchen-Aid beat for approximately 1 to 2 minutes. The mixture should not have any dry or crumbly bits.

Roll pie dough out on floured pastry mat, try to get it as thin as you can. Roll it into a rectangle.

Place the skinned sausages along the long edge of the pastry, end to end. Then start rolling up, gently! Once you have one layer around the sausages, stop rolling and cut along the edge. Use a dab or two of milk or water to make the pastry stick to itself and seal. Cut long wrapped sausage roll into sections, you can decide how big you want them to be, I usually do 3 to 4 inches. Then place these cut sausage rolls onto a parchment lined baking sheet.

Repeat with another row of sausages. Keep repeating until you have used up your sausage and/or pastry.

Once your baking sheet is full, brush the tops with milk and then bake in a 375°F oven for 10 minutes. Then turn the oven down to 350°F and bake for an additional 20 minutes.

Cooking time will vary depending on your sausage and oven. Make sure your sausage is fully cooked.

A Note: My husband loves sausage rolls. His love of sausage rolls has passed on to our kids!

It is something that I have not grown up with and there is just something about them that is not appealing to me, and I honestly have never tried ... but this book is our FAMILY cookbook of things we ALL love! ha! So, here's a recipe for all the sausage roll lovers!

I know they are good only because my family gobbles them up!

Enjoy!

"Cookery is not chemistry. It is an art. It requires instinct and taste rather than exact measurements."
--Marcel Boulestin

Shepherds Pie Spice Packet

Gluten Free

4 tbsps. Thyme, dried
1 tbsp. Garlic Powder
1 tbsp. Mustard, dried
2 tbsp. Basil, dried
1 tsp. Salt
1 tsp. Pepper

Mix the spices into a container with a sealed lid. Store until ready to use. Each time you are going to use the mixture, give the container a good shake and/or stir.

When making Shepherds Pie brown and cook 1 pound of ground beef and ½ of a chopped onion. Add 1 tablespoon tomato paste, 1 tablespoon gluten free worcestershire sauce, ½ cup beef stock, 1 tablespoon cornstarch and 1 ½ tablespoons of the spice mixture that you have made. Stir and simmer for 5 minutes. Put the hot meat mixture into a casserole dish or stuff your pepper jack-o-lanterns. Make mashed potatoes and put them on top of meat mixture. Bake at 375°F for 45 minutes to 1 hour.

A Note: My in-laws eat shepherds pie all of the time, it is a staple meal in their homes. I make it occasionally and nearly every halloween I turn the shepherds pie into 'Shepherds Pie Jack-o-Lanterns'.

When I was first diagnosed celiac, a prepackaged gluten free shepherds pie spice packet did not exist. Yet now you can easily find shepherds pie prepackaged spices in local stores.

I personally think that homemade is always better, but store bought is convenient and there is nothing wrong with just picking that up!

Enjoy!

Taco Seasoning

Gluten, Dairy & Egg Free

¼ cup Chili Powder
2 tsps. Garlic Powder
2 tsps. Paprika
2 tsps. Cumin
1 tbsp. Sugar
1/2 tsp. Salt
1 tsp. Pepper

Read your labels when purchasing spices, they are a common item to have gluten.

You can purchase gluten free taco packets from the store, yet they are more expensive than making your own. Also, if you make your own you know exactly what is in your spice mix and you can adjust the spice and taste to fit your likes. Plus, it is always my preference to purchase spices that are certified gluten free.

Put the ingredients into a small sealable container. Stir and then store in an airtight container and use when needed.

Add taco seasoning to browned ground beef, chicken, or turkey. The amount that you add will depend on how flavorful you like your meat. I would suggest adding 1 tablespoon to 1 pound of meat and then add more if you want more spice and flavor.

Enjoy!

Tortilla Chips

Gluten, Dairy & Egg Free

1 package Soft Tortillas, I use Grimms Gluten Free Corn package or La Tortilla Factory Gluten Free Ancient Grains Teff package
Olive Oil
Salt

Take a pastry brush and lightly brush olive oil on each side of the tortillas.

Sprinkle the tortillas lightly with salt. Cut each tortilla into 6 to 8 equal triangles.

Place them on a baking sheet. Make sure the pieces do not overlap.

Bake in a 350°F oven for 5 minutes.

Take pan out of oven and with tongs turn each tortilla over.

Return sheet to oven and bake tortillas for 7-10 minutes longer. Watch closely, as you don't want them to get too brown, just crispy!

Take out of oven when crispy and place pan on cooling rack.

The tortilla chips are great with salsa guacamole or with a bowl of chili! The chips can be eaten warm or cold.

Enjoy!

Yorkshire Pudding

Gluten Free

6 Eggs
¾ cup Milk
¼ cup Cream
¼ tsp. Salt
1 cup My Favourite 1:1 Flour Blend, in this book
1 tsp. Xanthan Gum
Canola Oil

If you are making roast for dinner, start your yorkshire pudding in the morning.

Put eggs, milk and cream into a blender and blend for 10 minutes.

Add salt, flour, and xanthan gum to blender and mix for 5 minutes.

Place blender into the fridge. Take the blender mixture out of the fridge and blend many times throughout the day for 5 to 10 minutes at a time. Remember to put the mixture back into your fridge between blending. One hour before you are going to start baking your Yorkshire puddings, take the mixture out of the fridge and blend 3-4 more times within that hour.

45 minutes before you are going to eat, turn on your oven to 425°F.

Then use a muffin tin that you don't care if it gets a bit messy. Pour canola oil into the bottoms of each muffin cup, about ¼ inch in each. Use your fingers to grease the sides and top of pan, then your Yorkshire puddings won't stick to the top of the pan.

Place the pan into the oven and heat until oil is sizzling, approximately 7-8 minutes. Be careful! As it is very hot, don't burn yourself or start a fire. When the oil starts to sizzle, carefully take out the pan and pour the batter into the hot oil, the cups should be ¾ full

Put pan back into oven and turn down the temperature to 375°F. Bake for 25 minutes. Do not undercook as they will be gummy and doughy. It would be better to overcook a bit than undercook!

Serve them immediately with sliced roast beef, mashed potatoes and gravy. Pour the gravy inside the Yorkshire pudding, it naturally makes a hole in the top when it bakes. When you cut into the Yorkshire pudding, it should collapse, this is how you know that you cooked it perfectly. If it is doughy, cook it longer next time. If it is crispy, cook it for a tad less time.

A Note: I grew up with my mom making roast on Sunday afternoons. She often made Yorkshire puddings with it as well.

She said the trick to great Yorkshire puddings is using more eggs and beating the ingredients in your blender throughout the day. The more you turn your blender on the bigger and better they will be. So, I listen to her and mine turn out fluffy, large and taste just like hers ... yet mine are gluten free style!

Enjoy!

"My mama always said, "Life is like a box of chocolates. You never know what you're gonna get."
--Forest Gump

Calzones

Gluten, Dairy & Egg Free

CALZONE DOUGH
2 cups Warm Water
1 tablespoon Instant Yeast
½ tablespoon Honey
½ tablespoon Maple Syrup
2 tablespoon Olive Oil

1 cup Brown Rice Flour
1 cup White Rice Flour
¾ cup Tapioca Starch
2 tbsps. Amaranth Flour
2 tbsps. Buckwheat Flour
1 ½ tsps. Dried Basil
1 ½ tsps. Oregano
1 ½ tsps. Garlic Powder
1 teaspoons Salt

3 tbsps. Chia (ground)
3 tbsps. Flax Meal
¼ cup Psyllium Husk (whole not powdered)

CALZONE FILLING
1 pound Ground Beef
1 jar Ragu Tomato Sauce
½ Onion, chopped
1 tbsp. Oil
2 cloves Garlic, minced
1 tsp. Basil
1 tsp. Oregano
Salt & Pepper, to taste
½ cup Fresh Mushrooms, sliced
1 jar Olives
1 cup Mozzarella, grated

CALZONE TOPPING
1 tbsp. Oil
2-3 cloves
1 pinch Red Pepper Flakes
28 oz Crushed Tomatoes, canned
Salt & Pepper, to taste
1-2 Fresh Basil leaves, sliced thin

Heat the oil in a frying pan and cook the onion on medium high heat for 2 minutes and then add garlic for 1 minute. Add the ground beef to the frying pan and brown meat until it is no longer pink. Then add the spices and tomato sauce. Simmer on low as you prepare the topping and calzone dough. Stir occasionally.

Now make your calzone topping. In a medium saucepan add the oil and sauté the garlic over medium heat, stir continually. Add the red pepper flakes, salt and pepper. Stir. Then add the tomatoes and basil and stir. Let this tomato mixture simmer on low while you make your calzone dough. Stir occasionally so that it does not burn.

Now you can make your calzone dough. In a measuring cup add water, maple syrup, honey, oil & yeast, mix gently. Set to the side.

In a Kitchen-aid mixing bowl add your rice flours, tapioca starch, amaranth flour, buckwheat flour, spices, and salt. Mix.

Add the chia, flax, and psyllium husk to the water mixture and mix well. Let sit for 60 seconds and then mix again with a spoon. Pour water mixture into the flour mixture and beat with Kitchen-aide for 3 MINUTES. Set your timer!

Preheat oven to 400°F.

Scrape dough onto lightly floured pastry mat. I use rice flour on mat. Cut the dough into 16 pieces. Roll each piece into a square (⅛ inch thick). Use a knife to cut the square into 4 equal squares and then put each piece onto parchment lined baking sheets. Repeat with all 16 pieces of dough.

Put a scoop of meat mixture onto the center of each calzone bottom. Then sprinkle mushrooms, olives and cheese on top of the meat. Leave some mushrooms, olives and cheese to sprinkle on top of the calzones. Do not over fill the calzones or they will be hard to seal.

Fold over the calzones and crimp shut around the edge.

Brush Calzones with a bit of olive oil and sprinkle lightly with cheese and/or mushrooms bits and/or olive pieces.

Bake in the oven for 25-30 minutes … take out and let each person pour sauce onto calzone or side of plate to dip. The sauce really makes the calzone extra delish!

This goes nicely with a fresh salad.

Enjoy!

"I have long believed that good food, good eating is all about risk"
--Anthony Bourdain

Another Great Recipe: _____
By: _____

Ingredients: Directions:
_____   _____
_____   _____
_____   _____
_____   _____
_____   _____
_____   _____
_____   _____
_____   _____
_____   _____
_____   _____
_____   _____
_____   _____
_____   _____
_____   _____
_____   _____
_____   _____
_____   _____
_____   _____
_____   _____
_____   _____
_____   _____
_____   _____
_____   _____
_____   _____
_____   _____
_____   _____
_____   _____

Notes:
_____
_____
_____

Another Great Recipe:_____
By:_____

Ingredients: Directions:

Notes:

Another Great Recipe: _____
By: _____

Ingredients: Directions:

Notes:

Notes

Recipes Sorted by Category

Breads & Muffins
Bagels *32*
Baguettes *35*
Banana Oatmeal Muffins *18*
Biscuits *15*
Cinnamon Buns *39*
Dad's Saturday Morning Waffles *17*
Flat Bread *30*
Garden Apple Muffins *19*
Blueberry Muffins *21*
Healthy Banana Loaf *25*
Lemon Poppy Seed Muffins *23*
Mini Cornbread Loaves *29*
Mom's Loaf *37*
Pumpkin Date Muffins *27*
Raspberry Muffins *28*

Cookies
Birds Nest Cookies *47*
Chewy Gingersnap Cookies *49*
Chocolate Chip Cookies *45*
Chocolate Sandwich Cookies *55*
Dan's Cookies *51*
Peanut Butter Cookies *54*
Hubby's Monster Cookies *51*
Royal Icing for Sugar Cookies *61*
Snickerdoodle Cookies *62*
Spice Cookies *57*
Sugar Cookies *59*

Desserts
Apple Cake *67*
Apple Pear Crisp *81*
Brownies with Naturally Flavored Raspberry Icing *82*
Butter Cream Icing *86*
Carrot Cake *87*
Cheesecake *95*
Cherry Cake *103*
Chocolate Cake (Easy) *85*

Desserts Continued
Chocolate Pudding *90*
Cream Cheese Icing *89*
Date Squares *91*
Donuts *69*
EASY Pineapple Upside Down Cake *105*
Gram's Raspberry Dessert *93*
Ice Cream Sandwiches *98*
Individual Blueberry Crisp *97*
Pavlova *104*
Pie - Mom's Flapper Pie *78*
Pie - Peach *75*

Pie - Pumpkin *77*
Pie Dough *73*
Pineapple Squares *101*
Plum Crumble *96*
Strawberry Rhubarb Cobbler *71*
Strawberry Shortcake *107*

Miscellaneous
Brown Flour *115*
Calzones *138*
Croutons *125*
Fish Sticks *119*
Games Night Dip *122*
Granola *127*
Granola Bars *123*
Mac & Cheese *112*
My Favorite 1:1 Gluten Free Flour *117*
Oven Baked Fries *121*
Pizza Crust *129*
Sausage Rolls *131*
Shepherds Pie Spice Packet *133*
Stuffing *113*
Taco Seasoning *134*
Tortilla Chips *135*
Yorkshire Pudding *136*

Recipes Sorted by Gluten, Dairy & Egg Free

Gluten & Dairy Free
Apple Cake - 67
Cheesecake - 95
Cherry Cake -103
Chewy Gingersnap Cookies - 49
Chocolate Chip Cookies - 45
Dad's Saturday Morning Waffles - 17
Dan's Cookies - 51
Fish Sticks - 119
Garden Apple Muffins - 19
Healthy Banana Loaf - 25
Hubby's Monster Cookies - 51
Peanut Butter Cookies - 54
Pie – Peach - 75
Pie Dough - 73
Pineapple Squares - 101
Pumpkin Date Muffins - 27
Royal Icing for Sugar Cookies - 61
Snickerdoodle Cookies - 62
Sugar Cookies - 59

Gluten & Egg Free
Biscuits - 15
Butter Cream Icing - 86
Chocolate Sandwich Cookies - 55
Cream Cheese Icing - 95
Great Gram's Raspberry Dessert - 93

Gluten Free
Bagels - 32
Banana Oatmeal Muffins - 18
Birds Nest Cookies - 47
Brownies with Naturally Flavored Raspberry Icing - 82
Carrot Cake - 87
Chocolate Cake (Easy) - 85
Chocolate Pudding - 90
Donuts - 69
EASY Pineapple Upside Down Cake - 105

Gluten Free Continued

Games Night Dip -122
Gram's Blueberry Muffins -*21*
Ice Cream Sandwiches-98
Lemon Poppyseed Muffins-23
Macaroni and Cheese -112
Mini Cornbread Loaves -29
Pavlova -104
Pie -Mom's Flapper Pie-78
Pie – Pumpkin – 77
Raspberry Muffins – 28
Sausage Rolls – 131
Shepherds *Pie Spice Packet - 133*
Strawberry Rhubarb Cobbler - 71
Strawberry Shortcake - 107
Yorkshire Pudding - 135

Gluten, Dairy & Egg Free
Apple Pear Crisp - 67
Baguettes - 35
Brown Flour - 115
Croutons - 125
Cinnamon Buns - 39
Croutons - 124
Date Squares - 91
Flat Bread - 30
Granola - 127
Granola Bars - 123
Individual Blueberry Crisp - 97
Mom's Loaf - 37
My Favourite 1:1 Gluten Free Flour - 117
Oven Baked Fries - 121
Pizza Crust - 129
Plum Crumble-96
Spice Cookies-57
Stuffing – 113
Taco Seasoning-   *134*
Tortilla Chips -   *135*

A Few of My Favourite Things

Friends and family have asked me where to find the following items for gluten free baking. In my opinion, I find them to be essential. I like to support locals, so see if you can find them where you are from. If you are not successful, then you can scan the QR code and order online. To be transparent, if you scan and order I will get a small credit for referring you. I only share the items that I use in my kitchen. I hope you enjoy these items as well and that they help make baking easier.

Scoops for muffins and cookies.

Rolling Pin/Pastry Mat that I use for my pie and cookies. I love the discs that you can change on the rolling pin to be able to roll out the dough evenly.

WHOLE Psyllium Husk can be hard to find. Make sure to not substitute for powdered.

WHITE Chia tastes the same as normal chia. I like to use in recipes because you can't see it.

My Christmas Cookbook full of family traditions gluten-free-style! Scan QR code to read more details and see the table of contents.

"If you can't feed a hundred people, then just feed one."
--Mother Teresa

www.glutenfreekob.com

www.ingramcontent.com/pod-product-compliance
Lightning Source LLC
Chambersburg PA
CBHW042229090526
44587CB00001B/3